Berlitz®

Englisch lernen mit Batman™

Bad Guys Gallery

Batman created by Bob Kane

Berlitz Publishing
München · New York · Singapur

Berlitz Englisch lernen mit Batman™ – Bad Guys Gallery

Vokabelerklärungen und Übungen: Astrid Stannat
Projektleitung: Eva Betz

www.dccomics.com
www.berlitzpublishing.de

Berlitz Publishing
Mies-van-der-Rohe-Straße 1
D-80807 München

Printed in Germany
ISBN 978-3-468-79407-0

1. 2. 3. 4. 5 11 10 09 08 07

Lieber Comic-Fan,

offensichtlich lieben Sie – wie Batman – Herausforderungen und wollen seinen Kampf gegen das Verbrechen und für die Gerechtigkeit im amerikanischen Original lesen. Sie werden Ihre Entscheidung nicht bereuen, denn mit den spannenden Geschichten frischen Sie auf unterhaltsame Weise Ihre Englischkenntnisse auf.

Damit Ihr Lesevergnügen nicht durch das Nachschlagen von unbekannten Wörtern beeinträchtigt wird, enthält dieser Comic-Band in regelmäßigen Abständen Ausklappseiten, auf denen Sie die deutschen Übersetzungen der wichtigsten englischen Wörter und Wendungen finden. Neben den englischen Vokabeln ist in eckigen Klammern die Aussprache in vereinfachter Lautschrift angegeben. Die erklärten Wörter beziehungsweise Textstellen sind in den Sprechblasen blau hervorgehoben. Die erste Ausklappseite finden Sie auf Seite 11. Klappen Sie sie einfach nach außen, und werfen Sie immer dann einen Blick darauf, wenn Sie auf ein Wort stoßen, das Sie nicht kennen.

Sollten Sie trotz der Vokabelerklärungen bei manchen Geschichten den Faden verlieren, dann lassen Sie sich nicht entmutigen: Auf den Seiten 115–118 finden Sie zu jedem Batman-Abenteuer eine kurze Inhaltsangabe, die Ihnen auf die Sprünge hilft.

Vielleicht haben Sie nach dem Lesen der Geschichten Spaß daran, Ihren Lernfortschritt zu überprüfen. Zu den einzelnen Episoden bieten wir Ihnen auf den Seiten 119–128 Kreuzwort- und Buchstabenrätsel sowie eine Reihe anderer kniffliger Aufgaben an. Durch die erneute Verwendung der Vokabeln werden sie noch besser im Gedächtnis verankert – und Sie können später leichter darauf zurückgreifen. Selbstverständlich sind auch die entsprechenden Lösungen im Anhang abgedruckt.

Viel Spaß beim Lesen!

Hinweise zur vereinfachten Lautschrift

Damit die Aussprache leicht nachvollziehbar ist, wurden bei dieser Lautschrift – von wenigen Ausnahmen abgesehen – Buchstaben aus dem deutschen Alphabet verwendet. Diese werden so ausgesprochen, wie Sie es vom Deutschen her gewohnt sind. Einige Besonderheiten sollten Sie aber beachten:

[ə]	arrive [əraiv]	gesprochen wie das kurze, unbetonte *e* in *bitte*
[ð]	the [ðə]	Das *th* wird wie ein stimmhaftes gelispeltes *s* in *Hase* gesprochen.
[θ]	three [θrih]	Das *th* wird wie ein stimmloses gelispeltes *s* in *Faß* gesprochen.
[v]	very [veri]	wie *w* in *wenig*
[w]	wine [wain]	wie *u* und *w* schnell hintereinander gesprochen
[s]	pleased [plihsd]	stimmhaft, weich gesprochen wie *s* in *sehen*
[ß]	street [ßtriht]	stimmlos, gesprochen wie *s* in *das* oder *ß* in *Straße*
[ai]	five [faiv]	wie *ei* in *mein* oder *ai* in *Main*
[äi]	say [ßäi]	*ä* und *i* schnell hintereinander gesprochen
[ou]	home [houm]	*o* und *u* schnell hintereinander gesprochen
[h]	student [ßtuhdnt]	hinter einem Vokal: lang gesprochen wie in *Stuhl*
	hand [händ]	vor einem Vokal: wie *h* in *haben*
ˈ	bedeutet, dass die nachfolgende Silbe betont ausgesprochen werden soll.	

COME ON...
TRUST ME.
SECOND TIMERS
SCOTT PETERSON Writer
TIM LEVINS Penciller
TERRY BEATTY Inker
LEE LOUGHRIDGE Colorist
ALBERT T. DE GUZMAN Letterer
HARVEY RICHARDS Assistant Editor
JOAN HILTY Editor
Batman created by Bob Kane

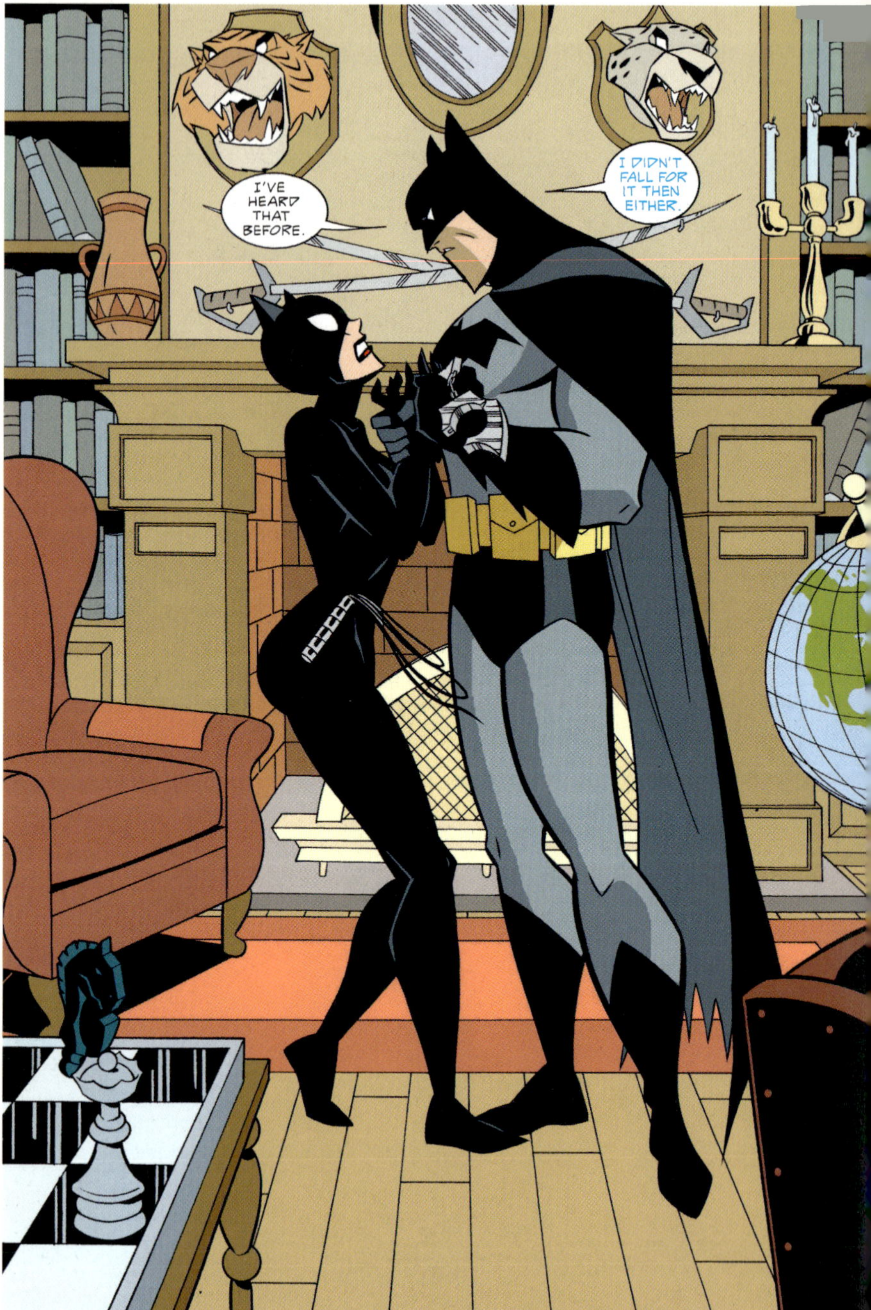
I'VE HEARD THAT BEFORE.
I DIDN'T FALL FOR IT THEN EITHER.

LISTEN, IT ISN'T WHAT YOU THINK THIS TIME.
IT NEVER IS, WITH YOU.
FINE.
KLIK
BE THAT WAY.
YOU'RE NEVER WILLING TO JUST--
AH, FORGET IT!

BUT YOU'LL HAVE TO EXCUSE ME, THEN.
AFTER ALL, I'VE STILL GOT WORK TO DO HERE.
HM?
OH NO.
TIK
TIK
TIK
IT'S A TRAP!

WHAT ARE YOU DOING?
YOU'VE GOT TO GET OUT OF--

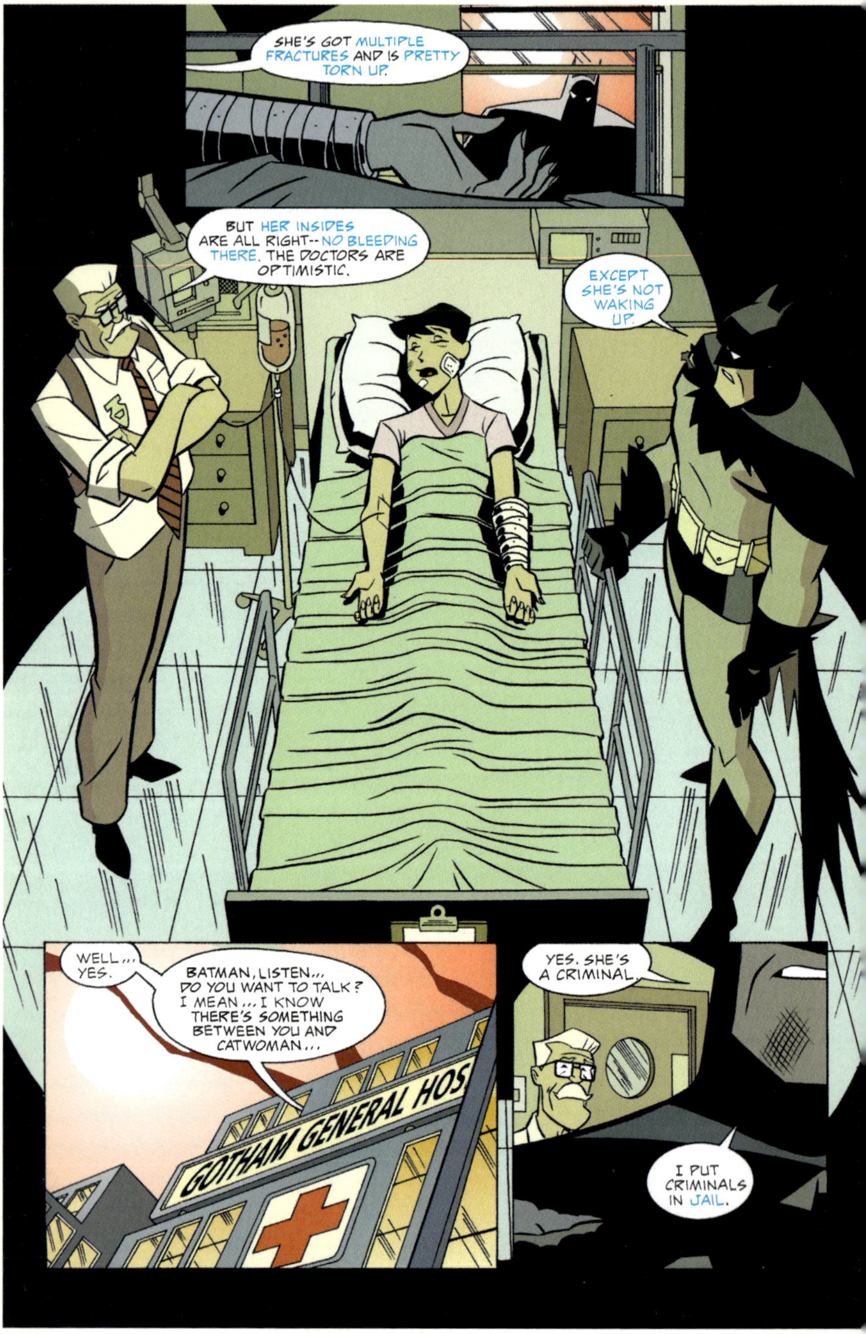
SHE'S GOT MULTIPLE FRACTURES AND IS PRETTY TORN UP.
BUT HER INSIDES ARE ALL RIGHT-- NO BLEEDING THERE. THE DOCTORS ARE OPTIMISTIC.
EXCEPT SHE'S NOT WAKING UP.
GOTHAM GENERAL HOS
BATMAN, LISTEN... DO YOU WANT TO TALK? I MEAN... I KNOW THERE'S SOMETHING BETWEEN YOU AND CATWOMAN...
WELL... YES.
YES. SHE'S A CRIMINAL.
I PUT CRIMINALS IN JAIL.

Vokabelerklärungen (S. 12–21)

S. 12/13

he's got no priors [hihs gat nou prairs] er hat keine Vorstrafen
was destroyed [wəs diˈßtroid] wurde zerstört
kind of an odd anti-theft device [kaind əv ən ahd ˈänti θeft diˈvaiß] eine ziemlich merkwürdige Diebstahlsicherung
she'd been lying low [schihd bin ˈlaiing lou] sie war auf Tauchstation
Any recent burglaries that might match this pattern? [eni ˈrihßənt ˈböhrglərihs ðət mait mätsch ðiß ˈpätərn] Irgendwelche kürzlich verübten Einbrüche, die mit diesem Muster übereinstimmen?
files [fails] Akten
but a bunch of rumors [bat ə bantsch əv ˈruhmərs] außer einem Haufen Gerüchte
apparently [əˈpärəntli] offensichtlich
a rash of [ə räsch əv] eine Serie von
for some reason, the victims aren't reporting them to the cops [fər ßam ˈrihsən ðə ˈviktims ahrnt riˈpohrting ðəm tə ðə kahps] aus irgendeinem Grund melden die Opfer sie nicht der Polizei

S. 16/17

alert [əˈlöhrt] Alarm
Defenses breached. [diˈfenßis brihtscht] Diebstahlsicherung durchbrochen.
Intruder detected on premises. [inˈtruhdər diˈtektid ahn ˈpremißis] Eindringling im Anwesen entdeckt.
impressive security [imˈpreßiv ßiˈkjuriti] beeindruckende Sicherung
You had some extraordinarily valuable items stolen recently. [ju häd sam ixtrohrdˈnerəli ˈväljubəl ˈaitəms ˈßtoulən ˈrihßəntli] Ihnen wurden vor kurzem einige außergewöhnlich wertvolle Gegenstände gestohlen.
insurance fraud [inˈschurənß frahd] Versicherungsbetrug
after bragging … about [ˈäftər ˈbräging … əˈbaut] nachdem ich … damit angegeben hatte
even outbidding … [ˈihvən autˈbiding] und sogar … überboten hatte
admit [ədˈmit] zugeben
humiliating [hjuhˈmiliäiting] demütigend

S. 18/19

coincidence [kouˈinßidenß] Zufall
him getting ripped off [him ˈgeding ript ahf] dass er abgezockt wurde
wealthy [ˈwelθi] wohlhabend
known for being less than fully compliant with the law [noun fər ˈbihing leß ðən ˈfuli kəmˈplaiənt wið ðə lah] bekannt dafür, dass sie sich nicht immer gesetzmäßig verhalten

S. 20/21

who won't be skimming off the top anymore [hu wount bi ˈskiming ahf ðə tahp eniˈ mohr] die nicht mehr das Beste absahnen wird
singed fur [ßindschd föhr] angesengtes Fell
to eavesdrop [tə ˈihvsdrahp] zu belauschen

▶ *Nächste Ausklappseite: S. 31*

WHAT HAVE YOU FOUND OUT?
UH... RIGHT. WELL, THEY FOUND THE OWNER OF THE HOUSE CATWOMAN BROKE INTO. HE WAS OUT FOR THE EVENING.
GOTHAM POLICE DON'T THINK HE HAD ANYTHING TO DO WITH IT. HE'S GOT NO PRIORS OR KNOWN CONNECTION TO CATWOMAN.
BESIDES, A LOT OF HIS HOUSE WAS DESTROYED-- KIND OF AN ODD ANTI-THEFT DEVICE.
WHAT WAS CATWOMAN EVEN DOING THERE? SHE'D BEEN LYING LOW FOR A LONG TIME NOW.
ANY RECENT BURGLARIES THAT MIGHT MATCH THIS PATTERN?
I'LL LOOK INTO IT. NOTHING'S POPPED UP YET.

OKAY, HERE'S SOMETHING.
I, UH, LOOKED INTO DETECTIVE MONTOYA'S FILES..THERE'S BEEN NOTHING OFFICIALLY REPORTED BUT A BUNCH OF RUMORS.
APPARENTLY THERE'S BEEN A RASH OF BURGLARIES LATELY BUT, FOR SOME REASON, THE VICTIMS AREN'T REPORTING THEM TO THE COPS.
GIVE ME A NAME AND AN ADDRESS.
OKAY! MY NAME'S TODD AND I LIVE AT--
NOT YOU.

ALERT. ALERT.
DEFENSES BREACHED.
INTRUDER DETECTED ON PREMISES.
IMPRESSIVE SECURITY, MR. BORODIN.
AN ALARM SYSTEM FIT FOR FORT KNOX. ENOUGH BODYGUARDS TO STOP A SMALL INVASION.
JUST NOT IMPRESSIVE ENOUGH.

YOU HAD SOME EXTRAORDINARILY VALUABLE ITEMS STOLEN RECENTLY. A PAIR OF PICASSOS. YET YOU DIDN'T REPORT IT.
WHY NOT? A LITTLE INSURANCE FRAUD, MAYBE?
NO! YOU... YOU COULD NEVER UNDERSTAND.
AFTER BRAGGING AT THE ICEBERG ABOUT FINALLY GETTING THE PICASSOS--EVEN OUTBIDDING MAURIZIO FOR THEM--
--HOW COULD I ADMIT THAT I, OF ALL PEOPLE, HAD BEEN ROBBED? DO YOU KNOW HOW HUMILIATING IT IS TO FIND YOUR SECURITY IS...
...WORTHLESS?
THE ICEBERG? DO YOU MEAN THE ICEBERG LOUNGE?
OF COURSE.
YOU... YOU WON'T TELL ANYONE THERE, WILL YOU?

HO HO. I'M SURE THAT'S A COINCIDENCE, HIM GETTING RIPPED OFF AFTER BOASTING AT A CLUB OWNED BY THE PENGUIN.
SEE IF ANY OF THE OTHER VICTIMS FREQUENTED THE ICEBERG LOUNGE.
LET'S SEE. ACCORDING TO MONTOYA'S NOTES, ALL THE VICTIMS WERE WEALTHY SINGLE MEN BETWEEN THEIR FORTIES AND SEVENTIES.
AND... YUP. THEY WERE EACH AT THE ICEBERG LOUNGE WHEN THE BURGLARIES HAPPENED.
WHAT'S MORE, MANY OF THEM ARE KNOWN FOR BEING LESS THAN FULLY COMPLIANT WITH THE LAW, IF YOU KNOW WHAT I MEAN.
LET'S GO HAVE A TALK WITH MISTER COBBLEPOT.

CATWOMAN
ELUDES G.C.P
STAKEOU

ICEBERG LOUNGE
WELL, LOOK WHAT THE CAT DRAGGED IN.
OR SHOULD I SAY, LOOK WHAT DRAGGED THE CAT IN.
WHY, IT'S MY VERY TALENTED BUSINESS PARTNER... WHO WON'T BE SKIMMING OFF THE TOP ANYMORE, WILL SHE?
I SEE YOU GOT MY MESSAGE. I TRUST YOU HAD TIME TO GET AWAY WITH LITTLE MORE THAN SINGED FUR.
WELL, YOU STILL HAVE EIGHT LIVES LEFT. AND AS LONG AS YOU REMAIN HONEST IN YOUR DEALINGS WITH ME--
FUNNY, I DIDN'T THINK YOU EVEN KNEW THE WORD "HONEST," PENGUIN.

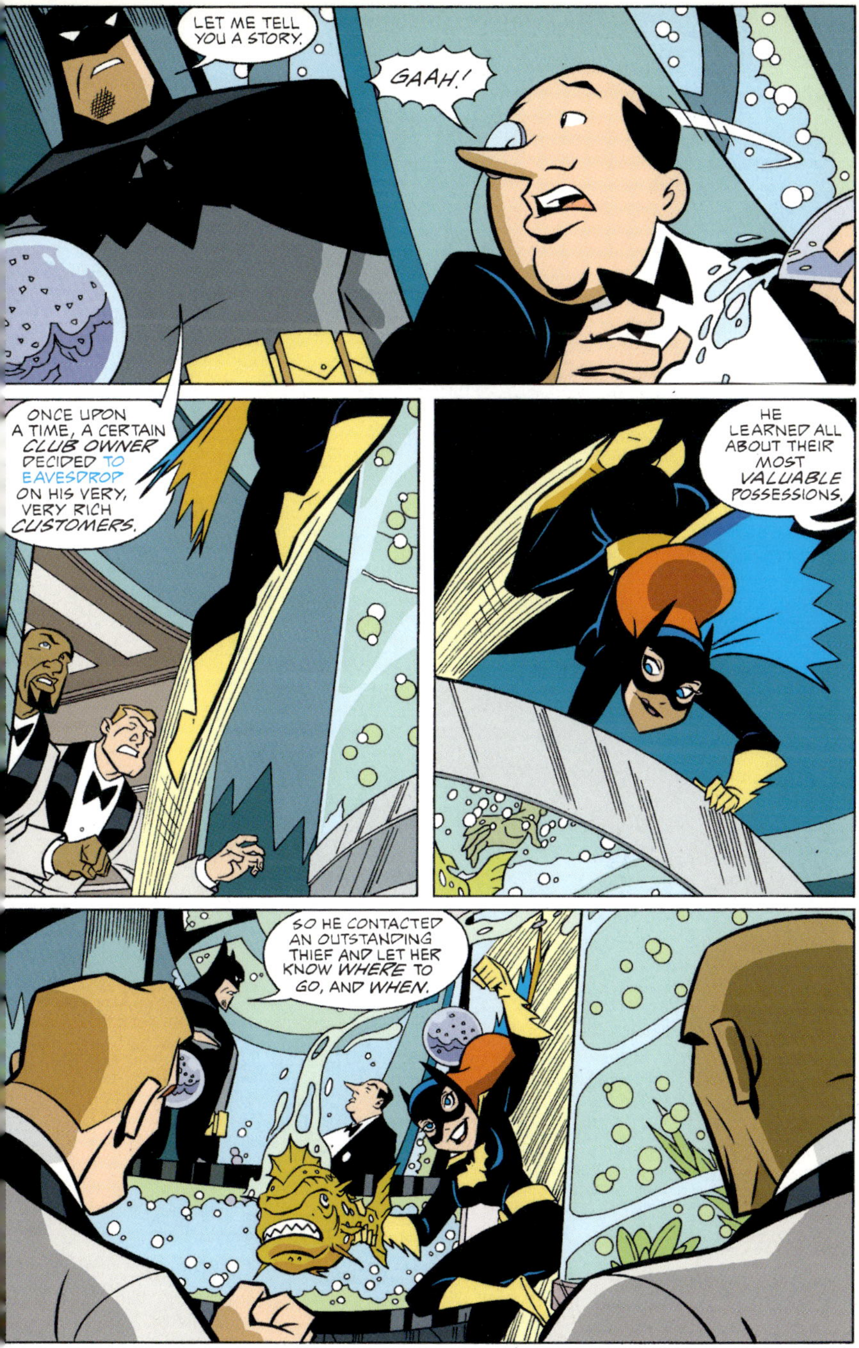
LET ME TELL YOU A STORY.
GAAH!
ONCE UPON A TIME, A CERTAIN *CLUB OWNER* DECIDED TO EAVESDROP ON HIS VERY, VERY RICH *CUSTOMERS*.
HE LEARNED ALL ABOUT THEIR MOST *VALUABLE* POSSESSIONS.
SO HE CONTACTED AN OUTSTANDING THIEF AND LET HER KNOW *WHERE* TO GO, AND *WHEN*.

THE CLUB OWNER KNEW THESE VICTIMS WOULD NEVER REPORT THEIR LOSSES, SO HE AND THE THIEF MADE OUT QUITE WELL.
UNTIL THE THIEF STARTING HOLDING BACK SOME OF THE LOOT. THE OWNER DIDN'T LIKE THAT... SO HE BLEW HER UP.
YOU CAN'T PROVE A THING WITHOUT CORROBORATION. AND I DOUBT THE KITTY-CAT'S GOING TO TESTIFY AGAINST HERSELF.
YOU'RE RIGHT. BUT IT DOESN'T MATTER. IT'S OVER.
BECAUSE IF IT'S NOT, I'M GOING TO TELL THE VICTIMS THAT SAME STORY.
WHAT EFFECT DO YOU THINK THAT WILL HAVE ON THE SCHEME? OR THE CLUB'S BUSINESS?
BUT THE CLUB OWNER SHOULD BE MORE WORRIED ABOUT WHAT THE THIEF IS GOING TO DO TO HIM. I SUSPECT HE'S GOING TO NEED MORE THAN NINE LIVES.

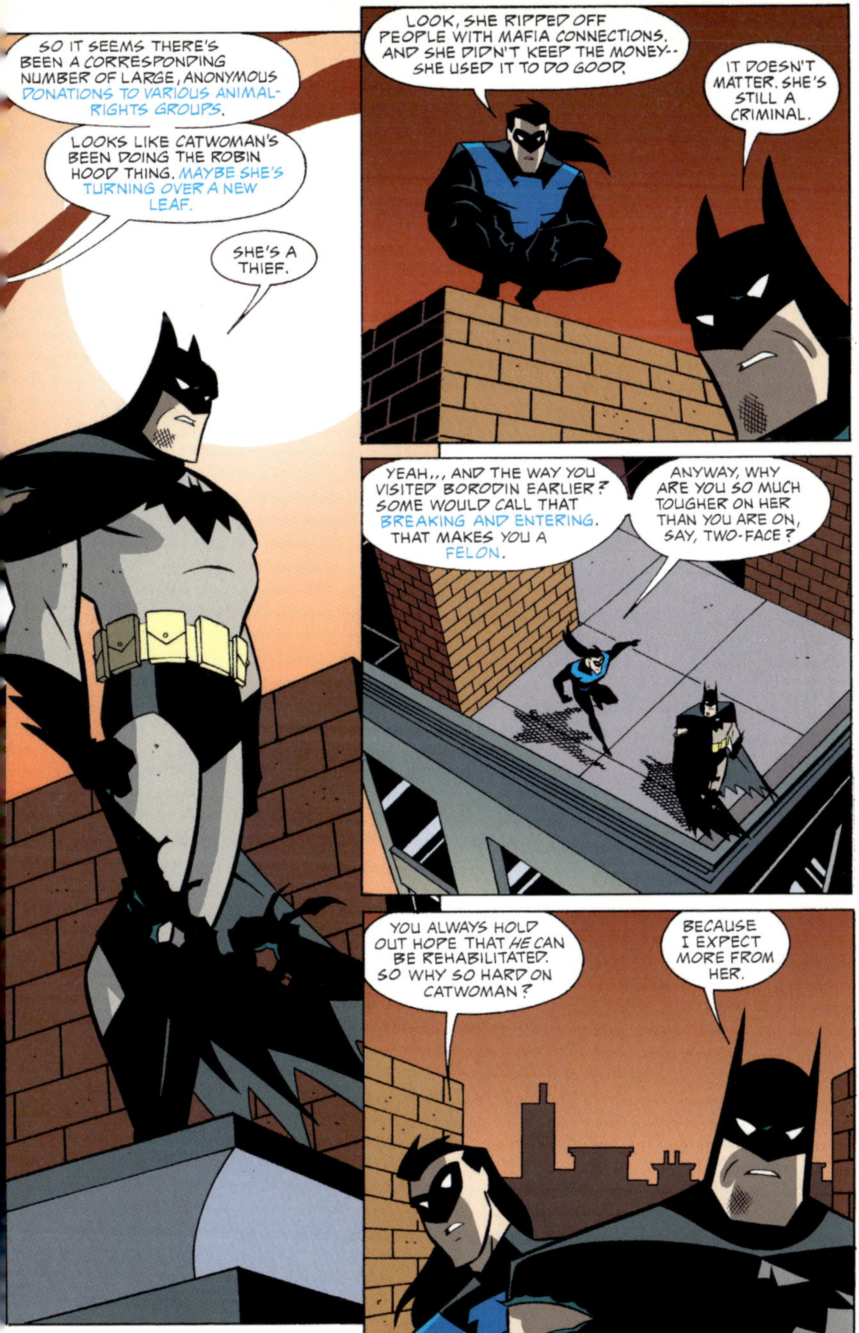
SO IT SEEMS THERE'S BEEN A CORRESPONDING NUMBER OF LARGE, ANONYMOUS DONATIONS TO VARIOUS ANIMAL-RIGHTS GROUPS.
LOOKS LIKE CATWOMAN'S BEEN DOING THE ROBIN HOOD THING. MAYBE SHE'S TURNING OVER A NEW LEAF.
SHE'S A THIEF.
LOOK, SHE RIPPED OFF PEOPLE WITH MAFIA CONNECTIONS. AND SHE DIDN'T KEEP THE MONEY-- SHE USED IT TO DO GOOD.
IT DOESN'T MATTER. SHE'S STILL A CRIMINAL.
YEAH..., AND THE WAY YOU VISITED BORODIN EARLIER? SOME WOULD CALL THAT BREAKING AND ENTERING. THAT MAKES YOU A FELON.
ANYWAY, WHY ARE YOU SO MUCH TOUGHER ON HER THAN YOU ARE ON, SAY, TWO-FACE?
YOU ALWAYS HOLD OUT HOPE THAT HE CAN BE REHABILITATED. SO WHY SO HARD ON CATWOMAN?
BECAUSE I EXPECT MORE FROM HER.

YEAH, WELL--
--NOT EVERYONE CAN LIVE UP TO YOUR EXPECTATIONS.
LISTEN...BRUCE... PEOPLE AREN'T ALWAYS WHAT THEY DO.
NO.
PEOPLE ARE EXACTLY WHAT THEY DO.
OKAY! WELL, CATWOMAN ALMOST GOT HERSELF KILLED TRYING TO SAVE YOU!
IS IT OKAY IF WE JUDGE HER ON DOING THAT?
GOTHAM GENERAL HOSPIT
AND I GUESS WE CAN JUDGE YOU BY WHAT YOU DO NOW?

MMM... OOH.
WHAT'D I DO LAST NIGHT?
WATER?
OH. IT'S YOU. LISTEN, IF YOU'VE COME TO--
NO. NO, I JUST... I JUST WANTED...
I JUST WANTED TO SAY THANK YOU.
I... I SHOULD HAVE TRUSTED YOU.
HUH.
YOU'RE WELCOME.
The End

THIS INSULT MUST STOP!
NO MORE BLURRING THE LINES!
NO MORE VIGILANTES!
LAW AND ORDER!
THAT'S HOW I RUN THINGS!
THIS IS MY TOWN NOW!
MY TOWN!
NO ASYLUM
TY TEMPLETON WRITER
RICK BURCHETT PENCILLER
TERRY BEATTY INKER
LEE LOUGHRIDGE COLORIST
PHIL FELIX LETTERER
HARVEY RICHARDS ASSISTANT EDITOR
JOAN HILTY EDITOR
BATMAN CREATED BY BOB KANE
GET THE MESSAGE, COMMISSIONER GORDON?
STAIRS

WHAT'S THAT? THE UMBRELLA SIGNAL?
IT'S NOT ENOUGH HE GOT ELECTED MAYOR? COBBLEPOT WANTS TO BE THE SUPER-HERO NOW?
COBBLEPOT for MAYOR
LAW and ORDER... FOR A CHANGE
ROYALE
COMPUTER.
DIAL COMMISSIONER GORDON'S OFFICE.
HELLO?
LOOKS LIKE PENGUIN IS KEEPING HIS CAMPAIGN PROMISE ABOUT ME...
I'VE GOT A BLACK-AND-WHITE ON MY TAIL.
UNIT 5607. OFFICER SPERLING, ISN'T IT?
HE'S NOT MUCH OF A DRIVER...
HOTEL
SCREECH!
...I DON'T WANT HIM TO GET HURT.
I...
I CAN'T DO ANYTHING ABOUT IT, BATMAN.
OUR NEW MAYOR MADE IT CLEAR HE CONSIDERED YOU AN OUTLAW ON THE DAY HE WAS SWORN INTO OFFICE.

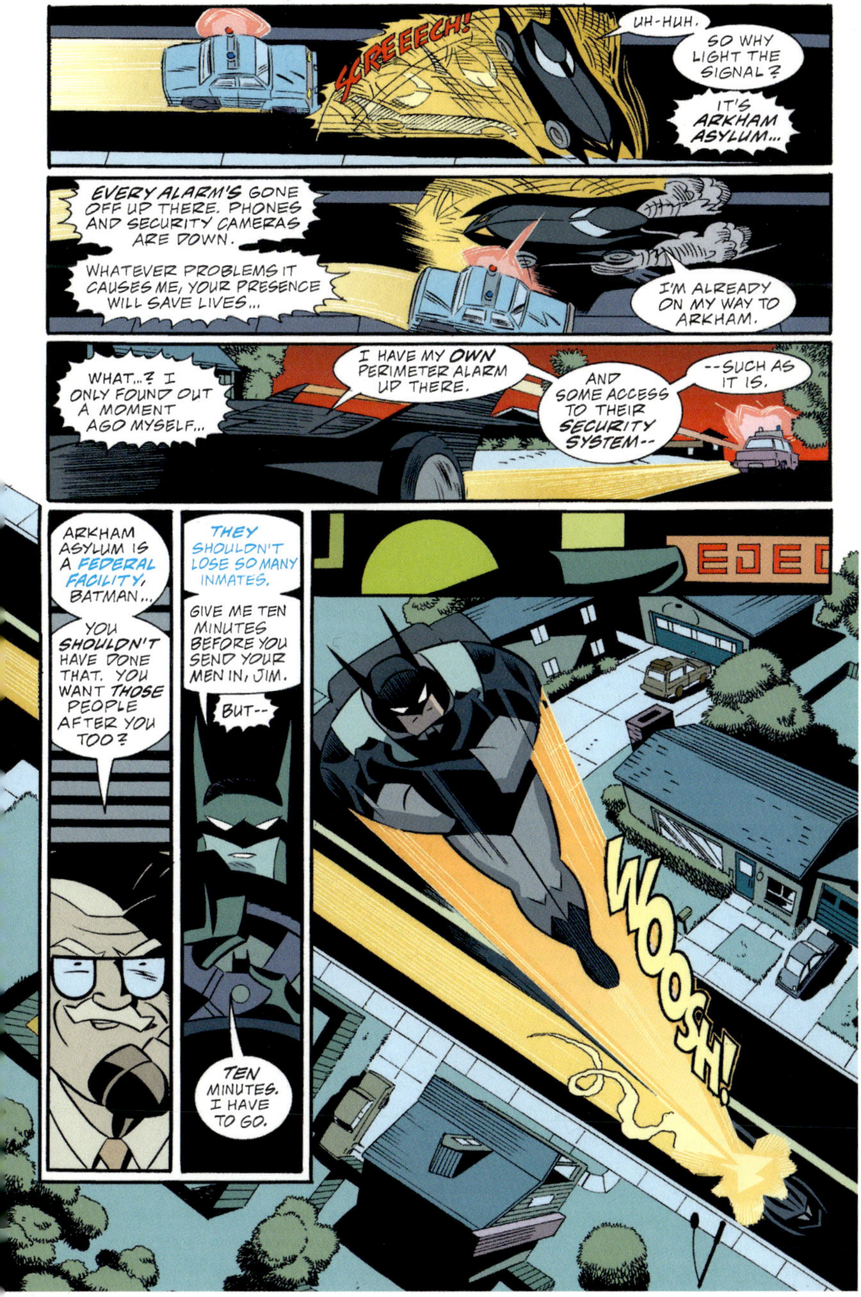
SCREEECH!
UH-HUH.
SO WHY LIGHT THE SIGNAL?
IT'S ARKHAM ASYLUM...
EVERY ALARM'S GONE OFF UP THERE. PHONES AND SECURITY CAMERAS ARE DOWN.
WHATEVER PROBLEMS IT CAUSES ME, YOUR PRESENCE WILL SAVE LIVES...
I'M ALREADY ON MY WAY TO ARKHAM.
WHAT...? I ONLY FOUND OUT A MOMENT AGO MYSELF...
I HAVE MY OWN PERIMETER ALARM UP THERE.
AND SOME ACCESS TO THEIR SECURITY SYSTEM--
--SUCH AS IT IS.
ARKHAM ASYLUM IS A FEDERAL FACILITY, BATMAN...
YOU SHOULDN'T HAVE DONE THAT. YOU WANT THOSE PEOPLE AFTER YOU TOO?
THEY SHOULDN'T LOSE SO MANY INMATES.
GIVE ME TEN MINUTES BEFORE YOU SEND YOUR MEN IN, JIM.
BUT--
TEN MINUTES. I HAVE TO GO.
WOOSH!

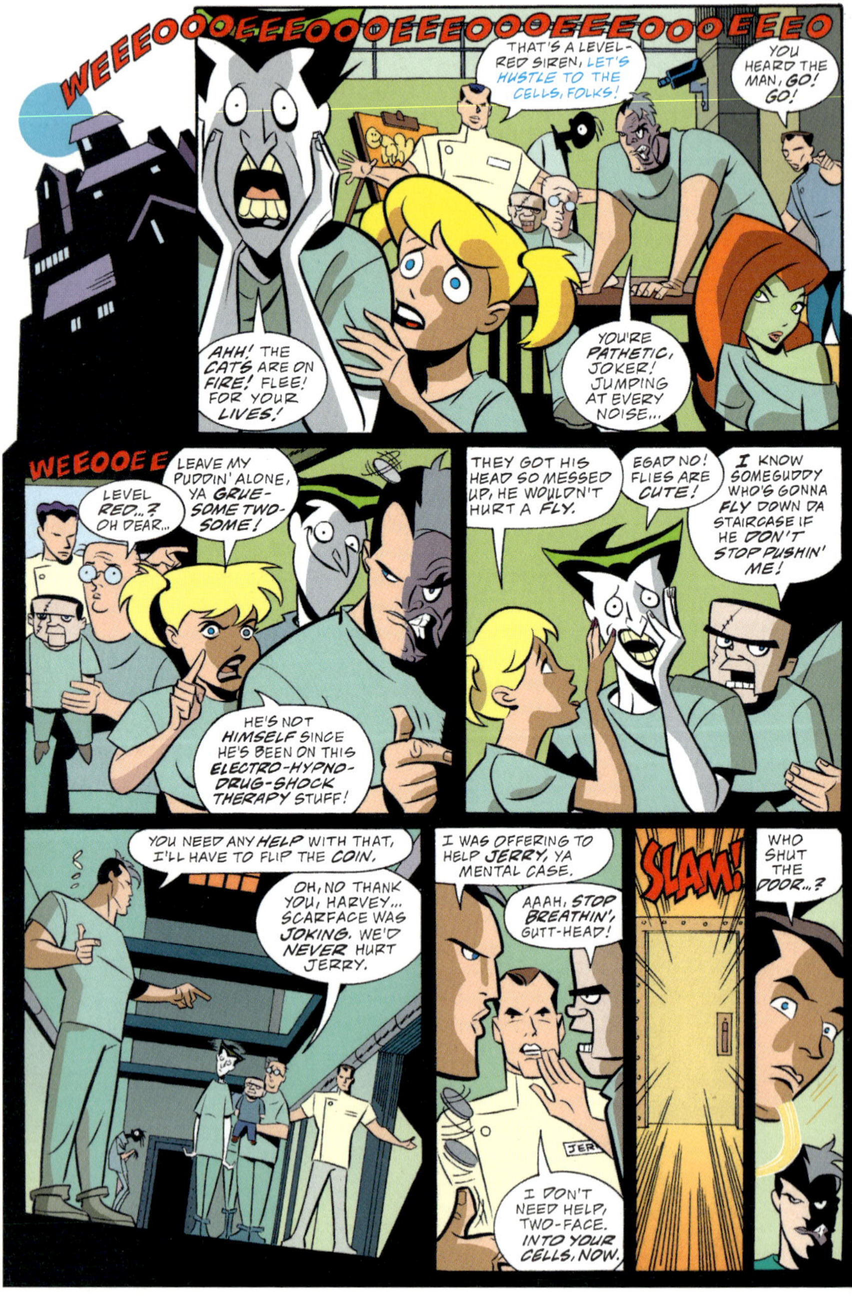
WEEEOOOEEEOOOEEEOOOEEEOOOEEEO
THAT'S A LEVEL-RED SIREN, LET'S HUSTLE TO THE CELLS, FOLKS!
YOU HEARD THE MAN, GO! GO!
AHH! THE CATS ARE ON FIRE! FLEE! FOR YOUR LIVES!
YOU'RE PATHETIC, JOKER! JUMPING AT EVERY NOISE...
WEEOOEE
LEVEL RED...? OH DEAR...
LEAVE MY PUDDIN' ALONE, YA GRUESOME TWOSOME!
HE'S NOT HIMSELF SINCE HE'S BEEN ON THIS ELECTRO-HYPNO-DRUG-SHOCK THERAPY STUFF!
THEY GOT HIS HEAD SO MESSED UP, HE WOULDN'T HURT A FLY.
EGAD NO! FLIES ARE CUTE!
I KNOW SOMEGUDDY WHO'S GONNA FLY DOWN DA STAIRCASE IF HE DON'T STOP PUSHIN' ME!
YOU NEED ANY HELP WITH THAT, I'LL HAVE TO FLIP THE COIN.
OH, NO THANK YOU, HARVEY... SCARFACE WAS JOKING. WE'D NEVER HURT JERRY.
I WAS OFFERING TO HELP JERRY, YA MENTAL CASE.
AAAH, STOP BREATHIN', GUTT-HEAD!
I DON'T NEED HELP, TWO-FACE. INTO YOUR CELLS, NOW.
SLAM!
WHO SHUT THE DOOR...?

Vokabelerklärungen (S. 32–41)

S. 32/33

bad guys [bäd gais] böse Jungs
Bad luck for the staff! [bäd lak fohr ðə ßtähf] Pech für das Personal!
that'll change [ðätl tschäindsch] das wird sich ändern
the innocents [ði ˈinəßəntß] die Unschuldigen
Do not harm … . [du naht hahrm] Tu … nichts.
That's up to the coin. [ðätß ap tə ðə koin] Das entscheidet die Münze.

S. 34/35

Clear the hall. [klir ðə hahl] Räumt den Flur.

S. 36/37

assassins [əˈßäßins] Killer
Who's made an enemy of this man? [huhs mäid ən ˈenəmi əv ðiß män] Wer hat sich diesen Mann zum Feind gemacht?
I've never heard of this Ghoul fella (= fellow) [aiv ˈnevər höhrd əv ðiß guhl ˈfelə] ich hab noch nie was von diesem Kerl namens Ghoul gehört
You're alive! [jur əˈlaiv] Du bist am Leben!
No kidding. [nou ˈkiding] Tatsache.
You're not even bleeding! [jur naht ˈivən ˈblihding] Du blutest nicht mal!
you keeping secrets from me [ju ˈkihping ˈßihkrətß frəm mih] dass du Geheimnisse vor mir hast

S. 38/39

What do you care? [wat du ju ker] Was kümmert es dich?
You're just trying ta (= to) change the subject! [jur dschaßt ˈtraiing tə tschäindsch ðə ˈßabdschekt] Du versuchst nur, das Thema zu wechseln!
When was this gonna (= going to) come up? [wen wəs ðiß ˈgənə kam ap] Wann wäre das zur Sprache gekommen?
big jerk [big dschöhrk] Volltrottel
Quite a halftime show. [kwait ə ˈhäftaim schou] Nette Halbzeit-Einlage.

S. 40/41

Keep your creepy hands off him! [kihp jur ˈkrihpi händs ahf him] Nimm deine gruseligen Hände von ihm!
I just saw my coin stuck under the wall. [ai dschaßt sah mai koin ßtak ˈandər ðə wahl] Ich hab gerade gesehen, dass meine Münze unter der Wand steckt.
Good side up. [gud ßaid ap] Die gute Seite nach oben.
until I can pry it loose [anˈtil ai kən prai it luhß] bis ich sie rausbekomme
That's a no-no! [ðätß ə ˈnounou] Das ist tabu!
Two of 'em (= them) ran past … that way. [tuh əv əm rän päßt … ðät wäi] Zwei von ihnen sind vorbeigelaufen … da lang.
searchlight [ˈßöhrtschlait] Suchscheinwerfer
We must leave! [wi maßt lihv] Wir müssen weg!

▶ *Nächste Ausklappseite: S. 51*

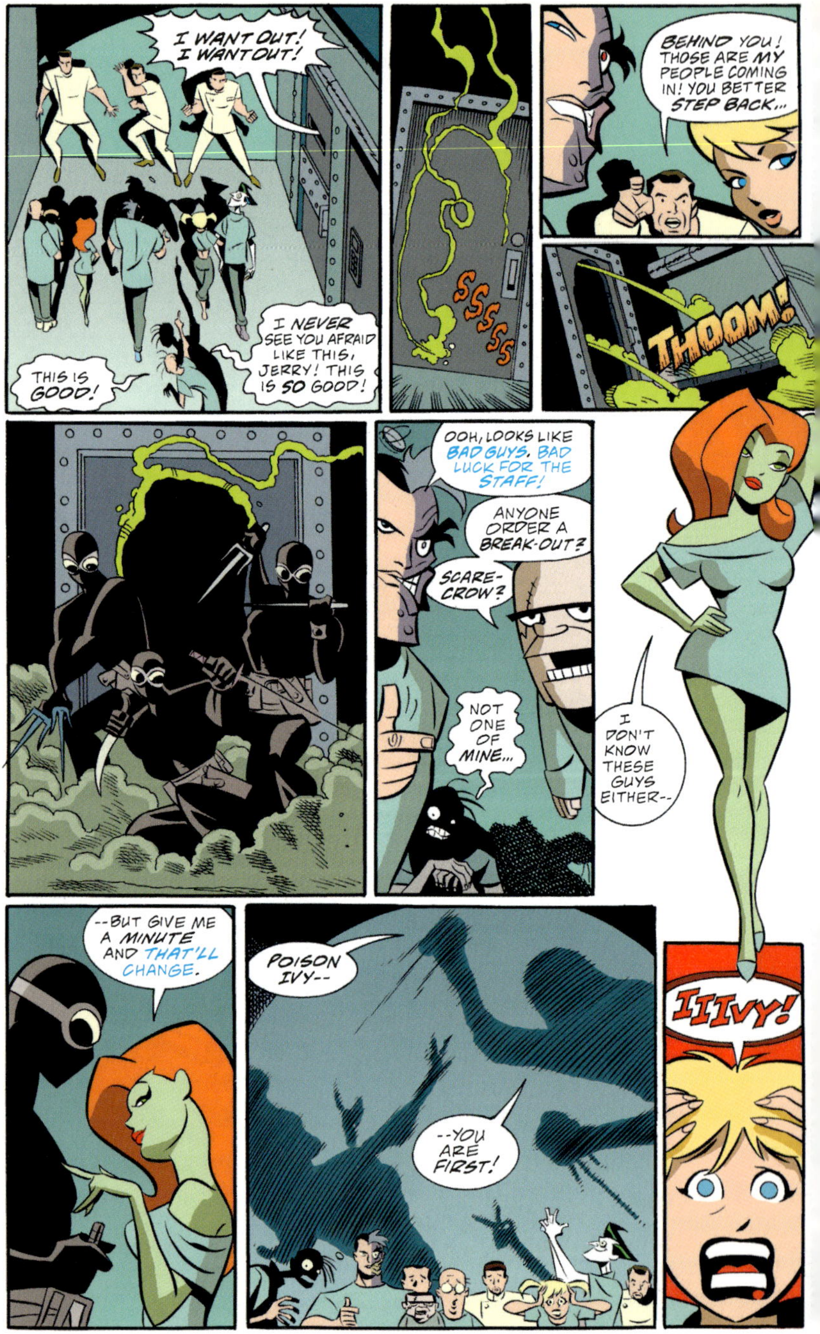
I WANT OUT! I WANT OUT!
I NEVER SEE YOU AFRAID LIKE THIS, JERRY! THIS IS SO GOOD!
THIS IS GOOD!
SSSSS
BEHIND YOU! THOSE ARE MY PEOPLE COMING IN! YOU BETTER STEP BACK...
THOOM!
OOH, LOOKS LIKE BAD GUYS. BAD LUCK FOR THE STAFF!
ANYONE ORDER A BREAK-OUT?
SCARE-CROW?
NOT ONE OF MINE...
I DON'T KNOW THESE GUYS EITHER--
--BUT GIVE ME A MINUTE AND THAT'LL CHANGE.
POISON IVY--
--YOU ARE FIRST!
IIIVY!

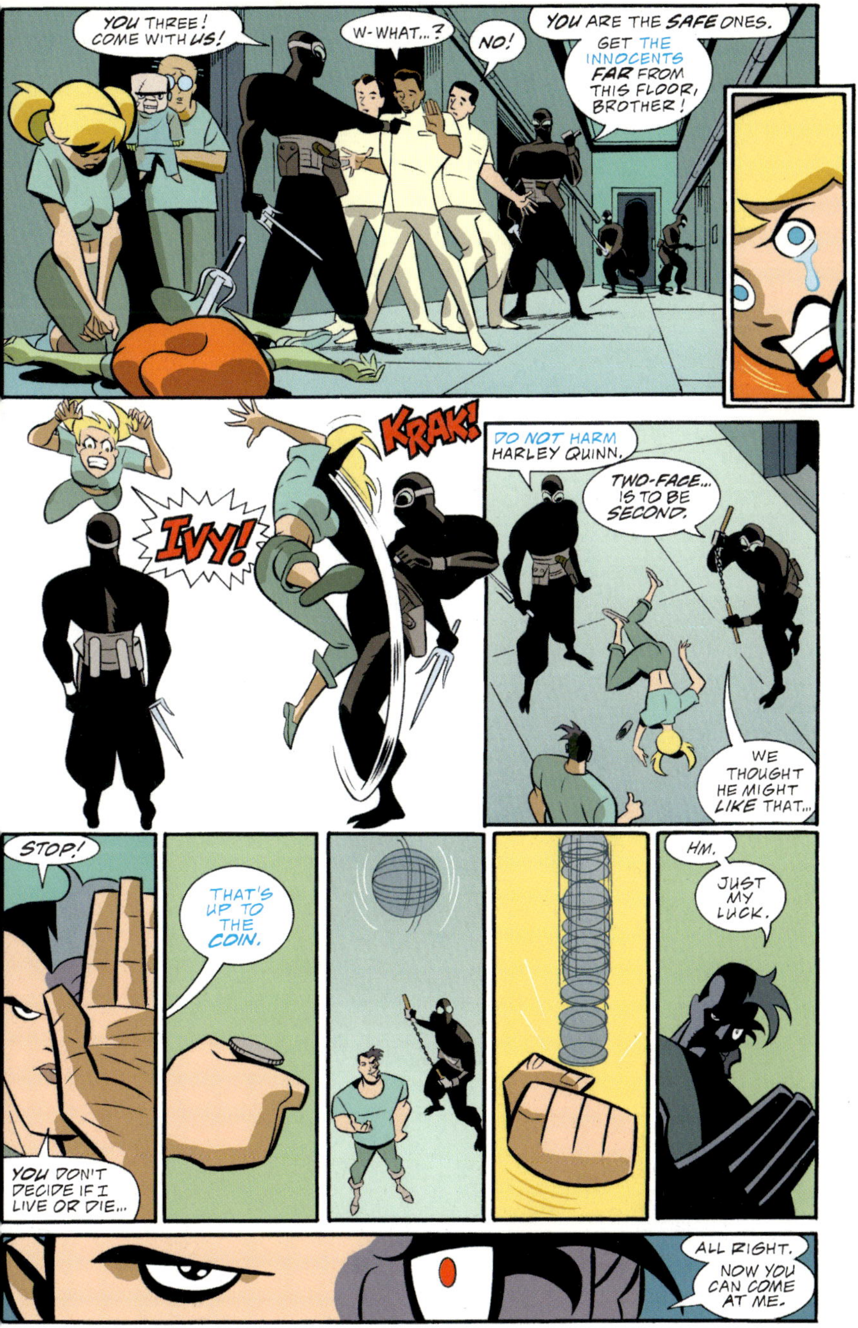
YOU THREE! COME WITH US!
W-WHAT...?
NO!
YOU ARE THE SAFE ONES.
GET THE INNOCENTS FAR FROM THIS FLOOR, BROTHER!
IVY!
KRAK!
DO NOT HARM HARLEY QUINN.
TWO-FACE... IS TO BE SECOND.
WE THOUGHT HE MIGHT LIKE THAT...
STOP!
YOU DON'T DECIDE IF I LIVE OR DIE...
THAT'S UP TO THE COIN.
HM.
JUST MY LUCK.
ALL RIGHT. NOW YOU CAN COME AT ME.

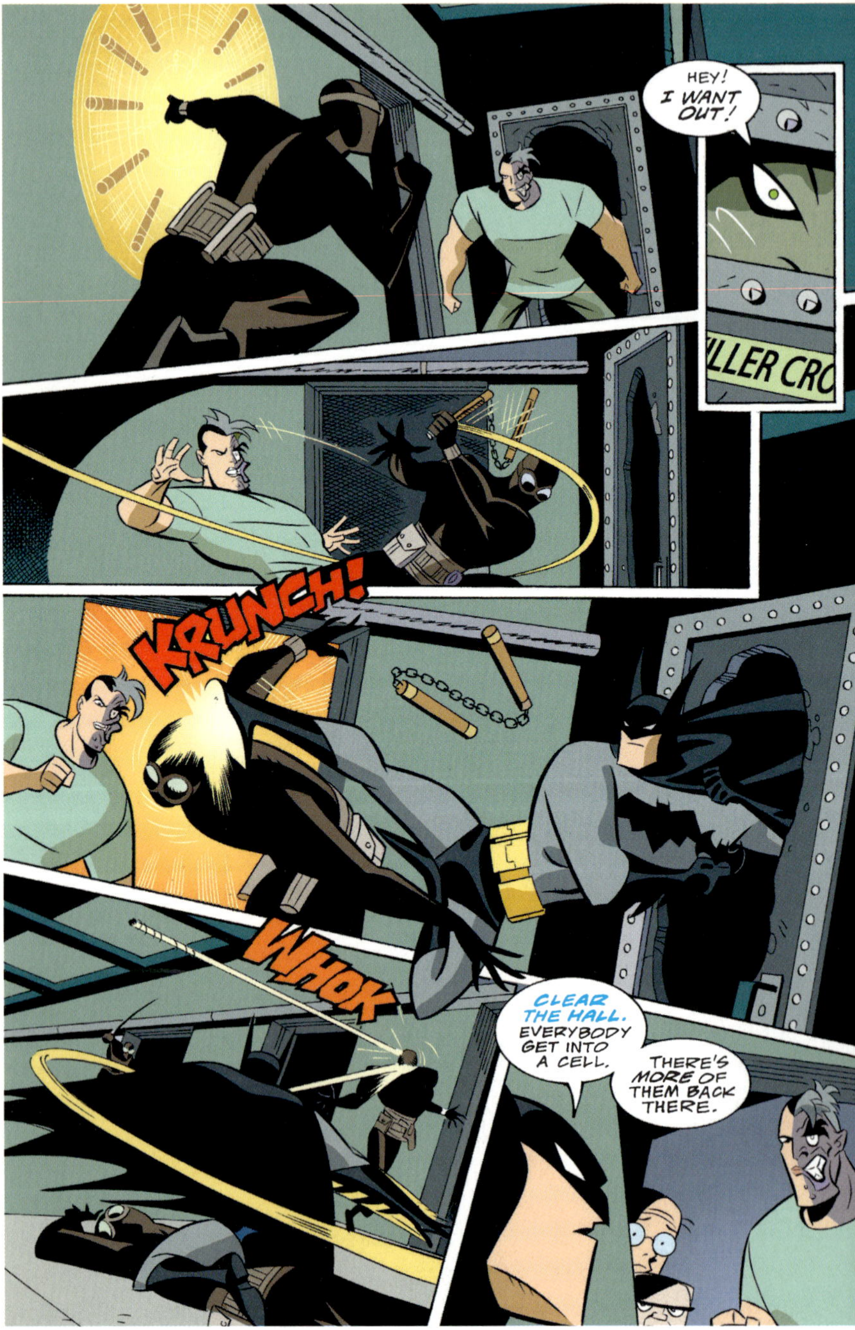
HEY! I WANT OUT!
LLER CRO
KRUNCH!
WHOK
CLEAR THE HALL. EVERYBODY GET INTO A CELL.
THERE'S MORE OF THEM BACK THERE.

FWOOSH!
HEY! I WANT OUT!
I WANT OUT!
KILLER CROC
OKAY, PEOPLE.
WHAM!
LET'S TALK.

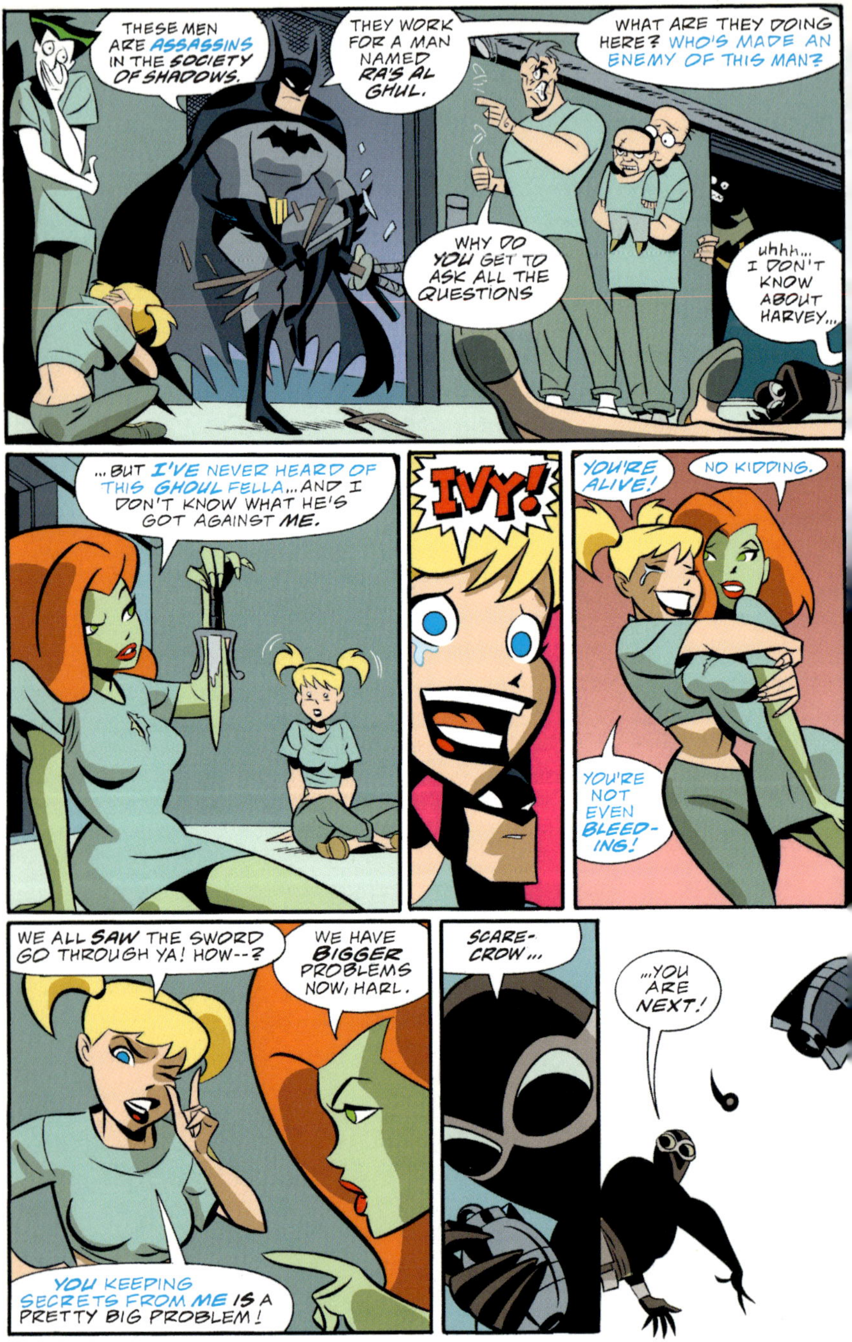
THESE MEN ARE ASSASSINS IN THE SOCIETY OF SHADOWS.
THEY WORK FOR A MAN NAMED RA'S AL GHUL.
WHAT ARE THEY DOING HERE? WHO'S MADE AN ENEMY OF THIS MAN?
WHY DO YOU GET TO ASK ALL THE QUESTIONS
uhhh... I DON'T KNOW ABOUT HARVEY...
...BUT I'VE NEVER HEARD OF THIS GHOUL FELLA... AND I DON'T KNOW WHAT HE'S GOT AGAINST ME.
IVY!
YOU'RE ALIVE!
NO KIDDING.
YOU'RE NOT EVEN BLEED-ING!
WE ALL SAW THE SWORD GO THROUGH YA! HOW--?
WE HAVE BIGGER PROBLEMS NOW, HARL.
YOU KEEPING SECRETS FROM ME IS A PRETTY BIG PROBLEM!
SCARE-CROW...
...YOU ARE NEXT!

I WANT OUT! I WANT...
SMASH!
...OUT?
HEY...
SSSSSSS
I'M...
...GOING...
OUT...

KABOOM!
HARLEY...
ARE YOU OKAY...?

THE...BOMB...
WHAT DO YOU CARE?
BOMB, SHMOMB. YOU'RE JUST TRYING TA CHANGE THE SUBJECT!
BEST FRIENDS TELL EACH OTHER THINGS...
...LIKE IF THEY GET A TATTOO... OR A NEW JOB...
WHERE IS IT? WHERE?
OR IF THEY'RE NOT REALLY HUMAN ANYMORE! WHEN WAS THIS GONNA COME UP?
YOU DIDN'T NEED TO KNOW. IT'S BEEN MY PROBLEM.
COULD YOU HELP ME...
...PLEASE.
HELP YERSELF, YA BIG JERK! YOU SHOULDA TOLD ME!
COME ON, MISTAH J!
IN A MINUTE.
MY, MY, MY. QUITE A HALFTIME SHOW.
NO, NO. DON'T GET UP, BATMAN...
THERE!
...YOU'RE A MAN WHO LOOKS GOOD WITH A HEAVY DOOR ON YOUR BACK!
JOKER...

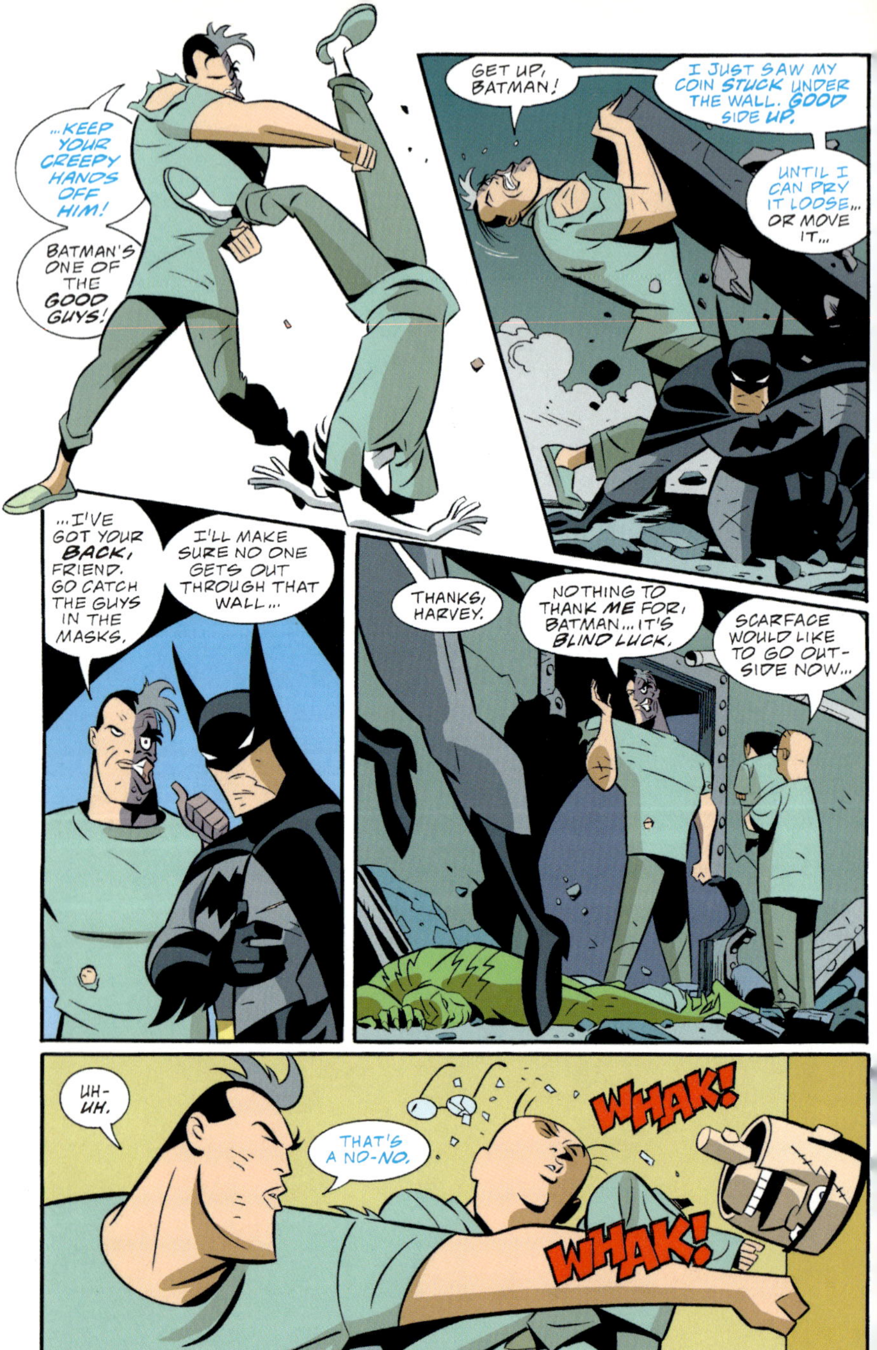
...KEEP YOUR CREEPY HANDS OFF HIM!
BATMAN'S ONE OF THE GOOD GUYS!
GET UP, BATMAN!
I JUST SAW MY COIN STUCK UNDER THE WALL. GOOD SIDE UP.
UNTIL I CAN PRY IT LOOSE... OR MOVE IT...
...I'VE GOT YOUR BACK, FRIEND. GO CATCH THE GUYS IN THE MASKS.
I'LL MAKE SURE NO ONE GETS OUT THROUGH THAT WALL...
THANKS, HARVEY.
NOTHING TO THANK ME FOR, BATMAN... IT'S BLIND LUCK.
SCARFACE WOULD LIKE TO GO OUTSIDE NOW...
UH-UH.
THAT'S A NO-NO.
WHAK!
WHAK!

ARE YOU ALL RIGHT?
YES... TWO OF 'EM RAN PAST... THAT WAY.
JUST NOW.
‹LOOK! BATMAN... IN THE POLICE SEARCHLIGHT!›
‹WE MUST LEAVE!›

WHOOOSH!
ALFRED.
SIR...?
I'M GOING TO NEED A PICKUP AT LOCATION KING BAKER SEVEN IN TEN MINUTES.
OF COURSE. WAS YOUR EVENING "ENCOURAGING" AFTER ALL, SIR?
NOT SO FAR...
...THANKS TO SOME BAD TIMING WITH THE POLICE.
PEOPLE GOT AWAY FROM ME.
FOR NOW.
POLICE

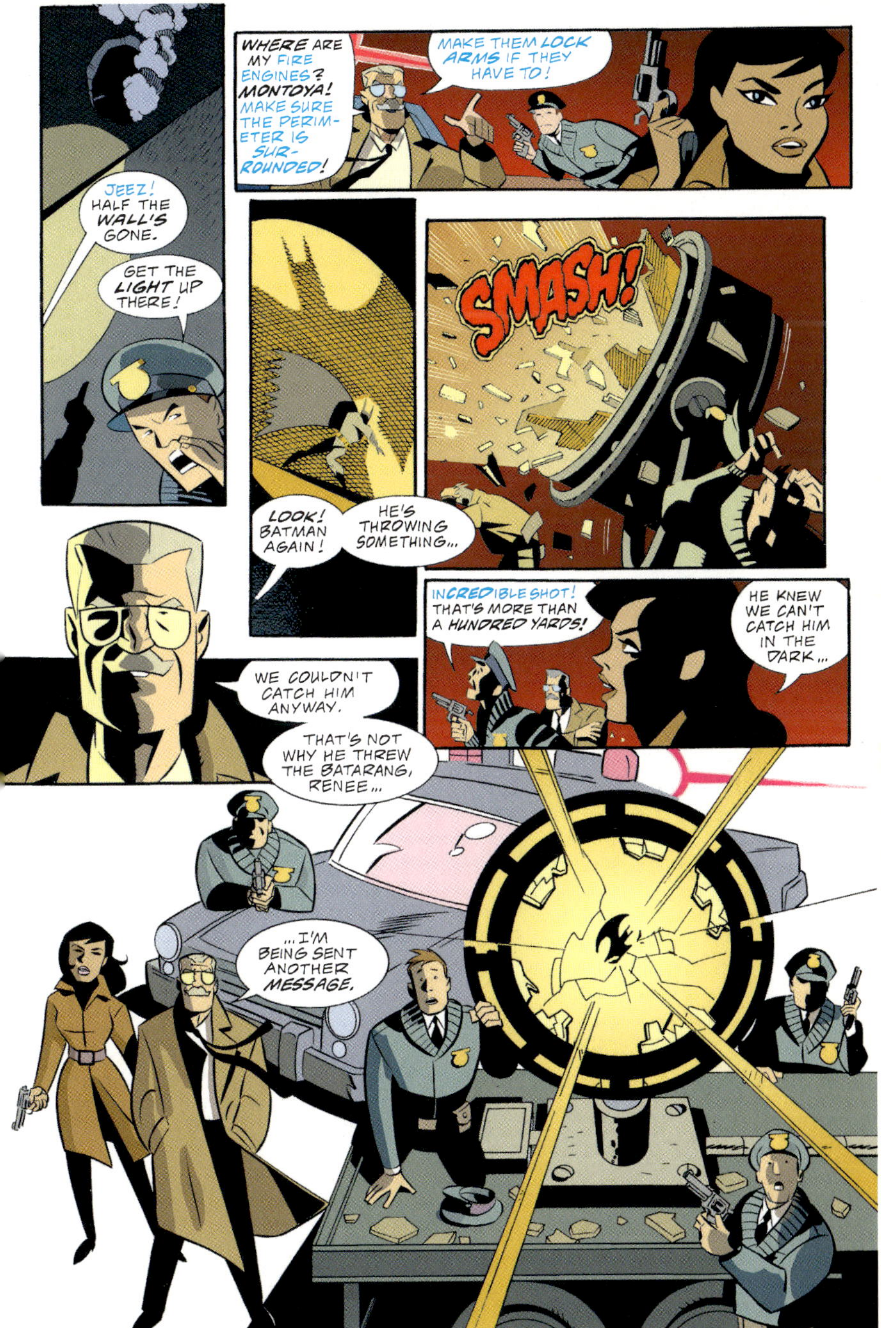
WHERE ARE MY FIRE ENGINES? MONTOYA! MAKE SURE THE PERIMETER IS SURROUNDED!
MAKE THEM LOCK ARMS IF THEY HAVE TO!
JEEZ! HALF THE WALL'S GONE.
GET THE LIGHT UP THERE!
LOOK! BATMAN AGAIN!
HE'S THROWING SOMETHING...
SMASH!
INCREDIBLE SHOT! THAT'S MORE THAN A HUNDRED YARDS!
HE KNEW WE CAN'T CATCH HIM IN THE DARK...
WE COULDN'T CATCH HIM ANYWAY.
THAT'S NOT WHY HE THREW THE BATARANG, RENEE...
...I'M BEING SENT ANOTHER MESSAGE.

IT WAS MY TURN TO PICK THE MOVIE.
THE MARK OF ZORRO.
HE WAS MY FAVORITE. MORE THAN SHERLOCK HOLMES, THE SHADOW, OR EVEN THE GRAY GHOST.
POP CORN
ZORRO
HE WAS BORN TO WEALTH, BUT HE PROTECTED THE POOR AND DEFENDED THE INNOCENT.
A DASHING CABALLERO, A MASKED MAN OF MYSTERY. A HERO.
ZORRO
THE MARK OF Zorro
I LOVED THE MOVIE. WE ALL HAD A GREAT TIME. BUT IT ONLY TOOK A MOMENT...
BANG!
HOWING TONIGHT
ZORRO
LINDA DARNELL
...TO BECOME THE WORST NIGHT OF MY LIFE.
OWN

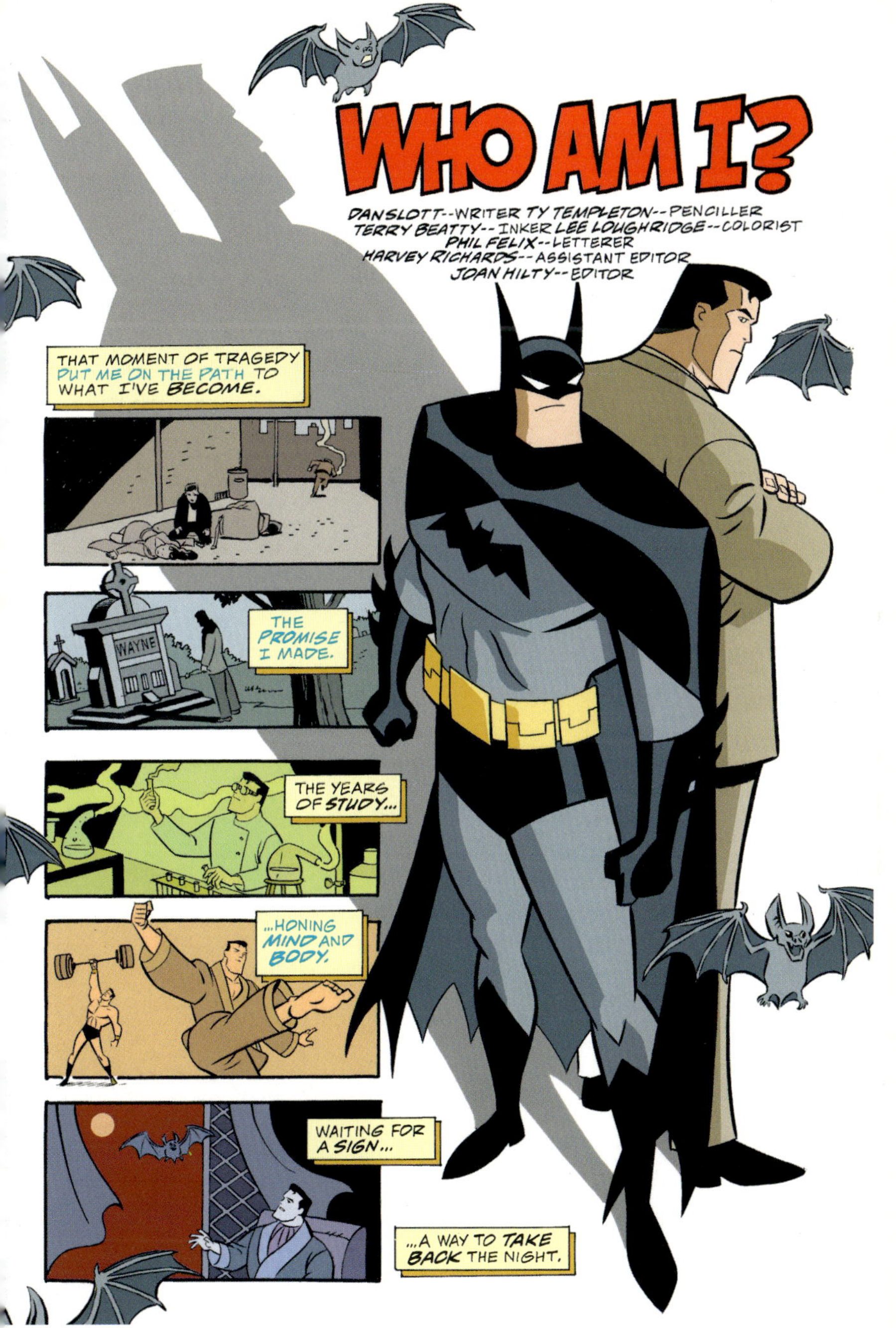
WHO AM I?
DAN SLOTT--WRITER TY TEMPLETON--PENCILLER
TERRY BEATTY--INKER LEE LOUGHRIDGE--COLORIST
PHIL FELIX--LETTERER
HARVEY RICHARDS--ASSISTANT EDITOR
JOAN HILTY--EDITOR
THAT MOMENT OF TRAGEDY PUT ME ON THE PATH TO WHAT I'VE BECOME.
WAYNE
THE PROMISE I MADE.
THE YEARS OF STUDY...
...HONING MIND AND BODY.
WAITING FOR A SIGN...
...A WAY TO TAKE BACK THE NIGHT.

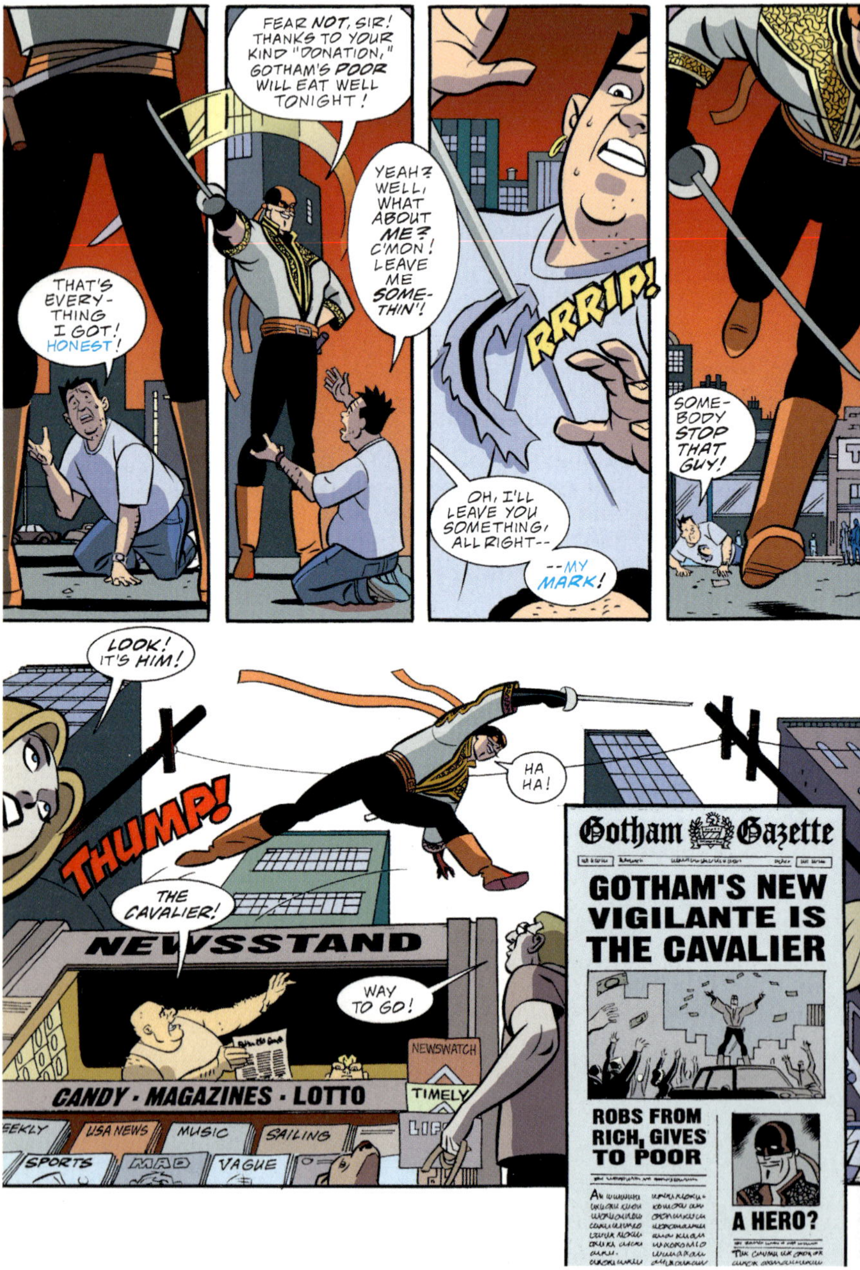
THAT'S EVERYTHING I GOT! HONEST!
FEAR NOT, SIR! THANKS TO YOUR KIND "DONATION," GOTHAM'S POOR WILL EAT WELL TONIGHT!
YEAH? WELL, WHAT ABOUT ME? C'MON! LEAVE ME SOMETHIN'!
RRRIP!
OH, I'LL LEAVE YOU SOMETHING, ALL RIGHT--
--MY MARK!
SOMEBODY STOP THAT GUY!
LOOK! IT'S HIM!
THUMP!
HA HA!
THE CAVALIER!
NEWSSTAND
WAY TO GO!
CANDY · MAGAZINES · LOTTO
NEWSWATCH
TIMELY
USA NEWS
MUSIC
SAILING
SPORTS
MAD
VAGUE
Gotham Gazette
GOTHAM'S NEW VIGILANTE IS THE CAVALIER
ROBS FROM RICH, GIVES TO POOR
A HERO?

HEY, CAVALIER! IN HERE, MAN!
WE GOT YOUR BACK, C!
Z
WEEEOOOO
AND ONCE AGAIN, THE CAVALIER SLIPS AWAY...
...THANKS TO HIS ADORING PUBLIC!
THAT'S QUITE A SCAM YOU'VE GOT!
BATMAN!
SWISH!
...AND KEEPING MOST FOR YOURSELF!
YOUR PAYOFFS MAY ENDEAR YOU TO THE STREET SCUM OF GOTHAM--
WAK!
ROBBING FROM THE RICH, GIVING TO THE POOR...
--BUT NOT TO ME.
YOU'RE NOTHING MORE THAN A COMMON THIEF.

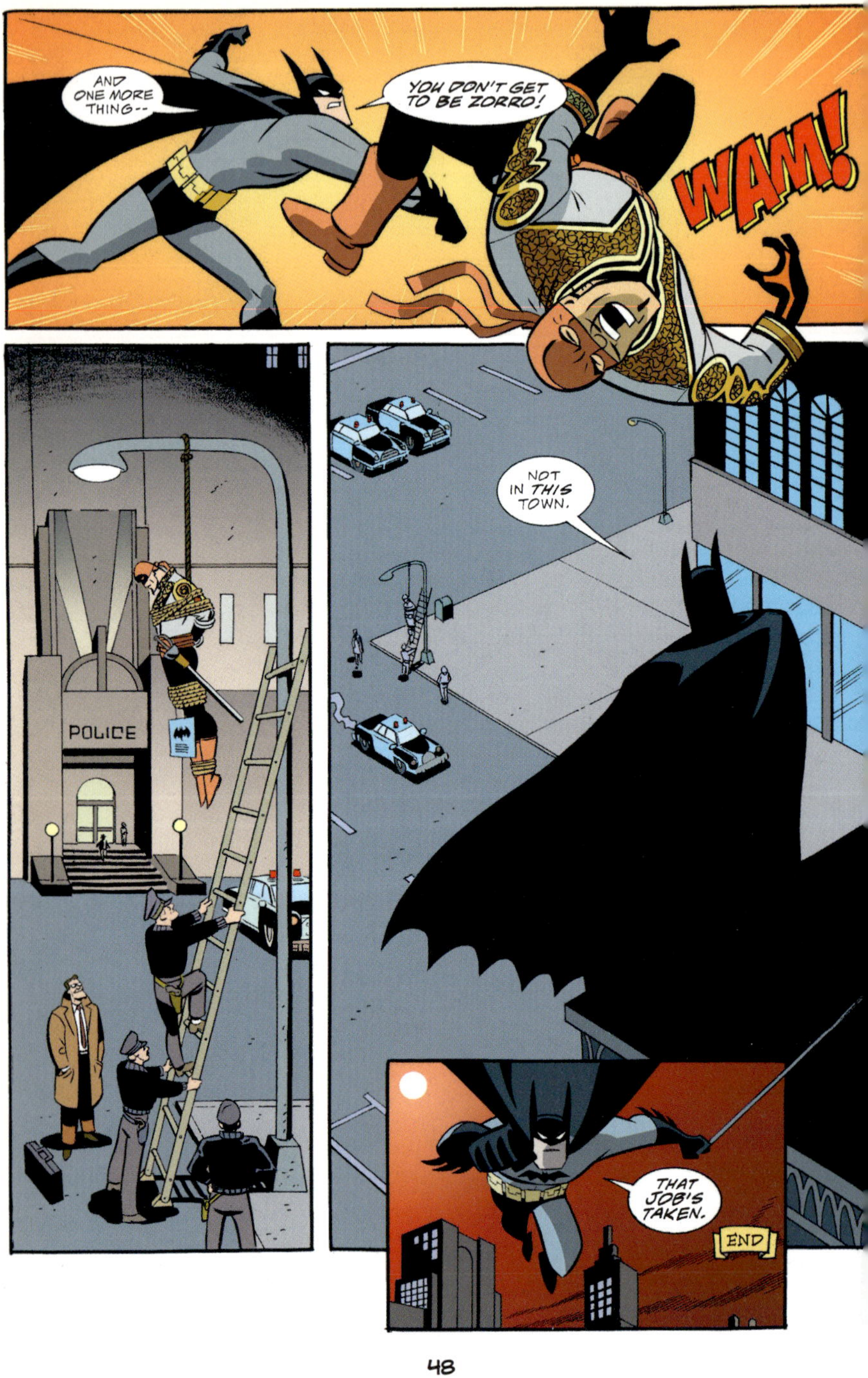
AND ONE MORE THING--
YOU DON'T GET TO BE ZORRO!
WAM!
POLICE
NOT IN THIS TOWN.
THAT JOB'S TAKEN.
END

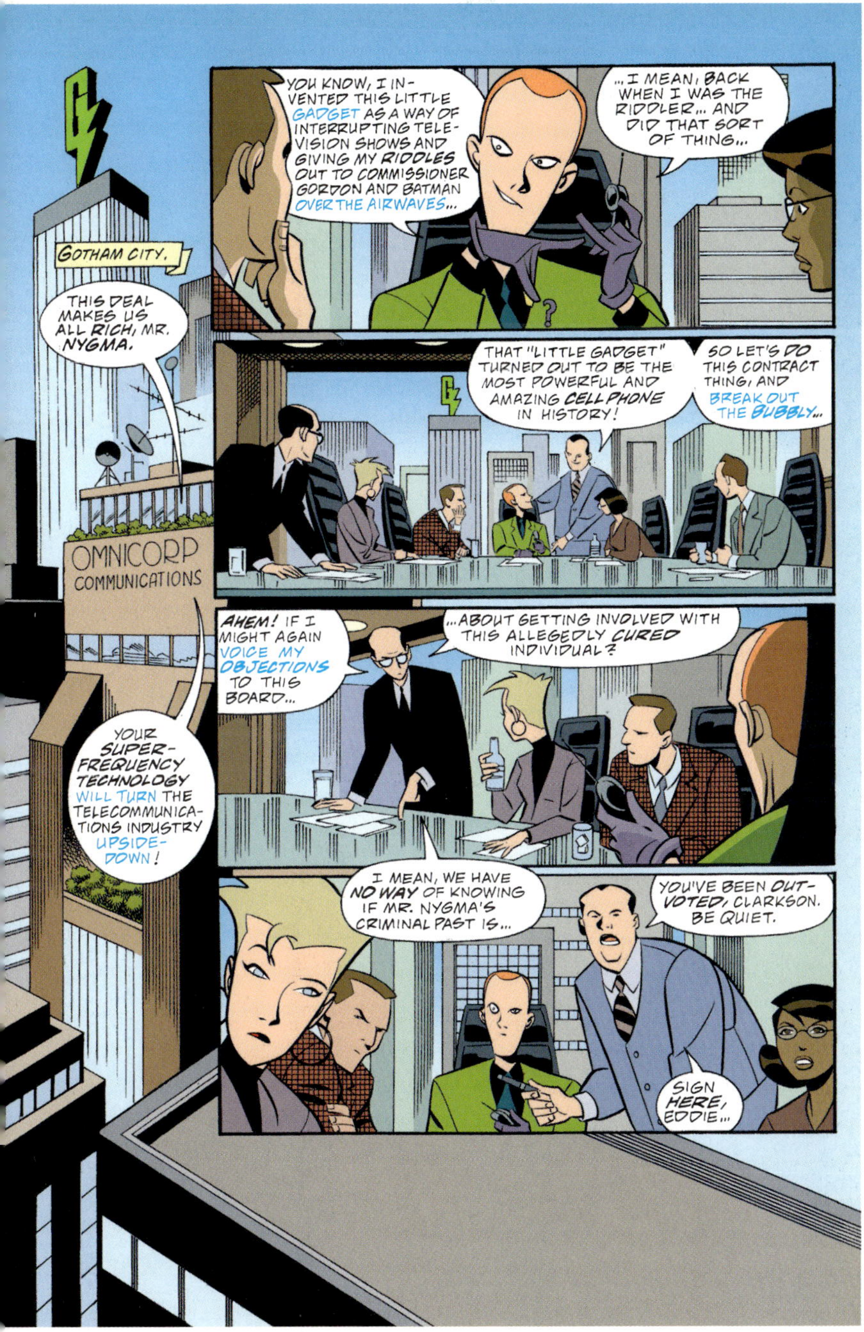
GOTHAM CITY.
THIS DEAL MAKES US ALL RICH, MR. NYGMA.
YOUR SUPER-FREQUENCY TECHNOLOGY WILL TURN THE TELECOMMUNICATIONS INDUSTRY UPSIDE-DOWN!
YOU KNOW, I INVENTED THIS LITTLE GADGET AS A WAY OF INTERRUPTING TELEVISION SHOWS AND GIVING MY RIDDLES OUT TO COMMISSIONER GORDON AND BATMAN OVER THE AIRWAVES...
...I MEAN, BACK WHEN I WAS THE RIDDLER... AND DID THAT SORT OF THING...
THAT "LITTLE GADGET" TURNED OUT TO BE THE MOST POWERFUL AND AMAZING CELL PHONE IN HISTORY!
SO LET'S DO THIS CONTRACT THING, AND BREAK OUT THE BUBBLY...
OMNICORP COMMUNICATIONS
AHEM! IF I MIGHT AGAIN VOICE MY OBJECTIONS TO THIS BOARD...
...ABOUT GETTING INVOLVED WITH THIS ALLEGEDLY CURED INDIVIDUAL?
I MEAN, WE HAVE NO WAY OF KNOWING IF MR. NYGMA'S CRIMINAL PAST IS...
YOU'VE BEEN OUT-VOTED, CLARKSON. BE QUIET.
SIGN HERE, EDDIE...

EVERYBODY DOWN!
EXCEPT FOR YOU, EDWARD NYGMA...
YOU HAVE TO DIE!
KABLAM!
AND WHO ARE YOU GUYS SUPPOSED TO BE?!?
WHAK!

Vokabelerklärungen (S. 52–61)

S. 52/53

three dates in a row [θrih däitß in ə rou] drei Verabredungen hintereinander
without somebody dishing about you [wiðˈaut ˈßambadi ˈdisching əˈbaut ju] ohne dass jemand Geschichten über dich auftischt
all of a sudden [ahl əv ə ßadn] auf einmal
eagle eye [ˈihgəl ai] Adlerauge
littering ad [ˈlitəring äd] Werbeplakat zum Thema Müll
I can't imagine why [ai känt iˈmädschin wai] ich kann mir nicht vorstellen, warum
in that bunch [in ðät bantsch] in diesem Haufen
you're getting so worked up [jur ˈgeding ßou wöhrkt ap] du regst dich so auf
gawky Gothamites [ˈgahki ˈgoθəmaitß] ihr einfältigen Bewohner von Gotham
rescue time [ˈreßkju taim] Zeit für einen Rettungseinsatz

S. 54/55

It's not even difficult. [itß naht ˈivən ˈdifikəlt] Es ist nicht mal schwierig.
dozens [ˈdasəns] Dutzende
if I can't triangulate the source of that signal [if ai känt traiˈängjuläit ðə ßohrß əv ðät ˈßignəl] ob ich nicht den Ausgangspunkt des Signals lokalisieren kann
unless you prefer to stay … [anˈleß ju priˈföhr tə ßtäi] es sei denn, Sie ziehen es vor … zu bleiben
start praying [ßtahrt ˈpräiing] fang an zu beten

S. 56/57

crossfire [ˈkrahßfair] Kreuzfeuer
shut up [schat ap] halt den Mund
Not if I can help it! [naht if ai kən help it] Nicht wenn ich es verhindern kann!

S. 58/59

fancy-pants [ˈfänßi päntß] Klugscheißer/du mit der aparten Hose
a place to hide [ə pläiß tə haid] einen Ort, wo du dich verstecken kannst
has targeted … [həs ˈtahrgitid] hat … ins Visier genommen
to solve it [tə ßahlv it] um es zu lösen
why gamble your life [wai ˈgämbəl jur laif] warum setzt du dein Leben aufs Spiel

S. 60/61

he incapacitated … [hi inkəˈpäßətäitid] er hat … außer Gefecht gesetzt
before either of us could withdraw [biˈfohr ˈihðər əv aß kud wiðˈdrah] bevor wir uns beide zurückziehen konnten
assignment [əˈßainmənt] Auftrag
rent a room [rent ə ruhm] ein Zimmer mieten
juice [dschuhß] Saft

▶ *Nächste Ausklappseite: S. 71*

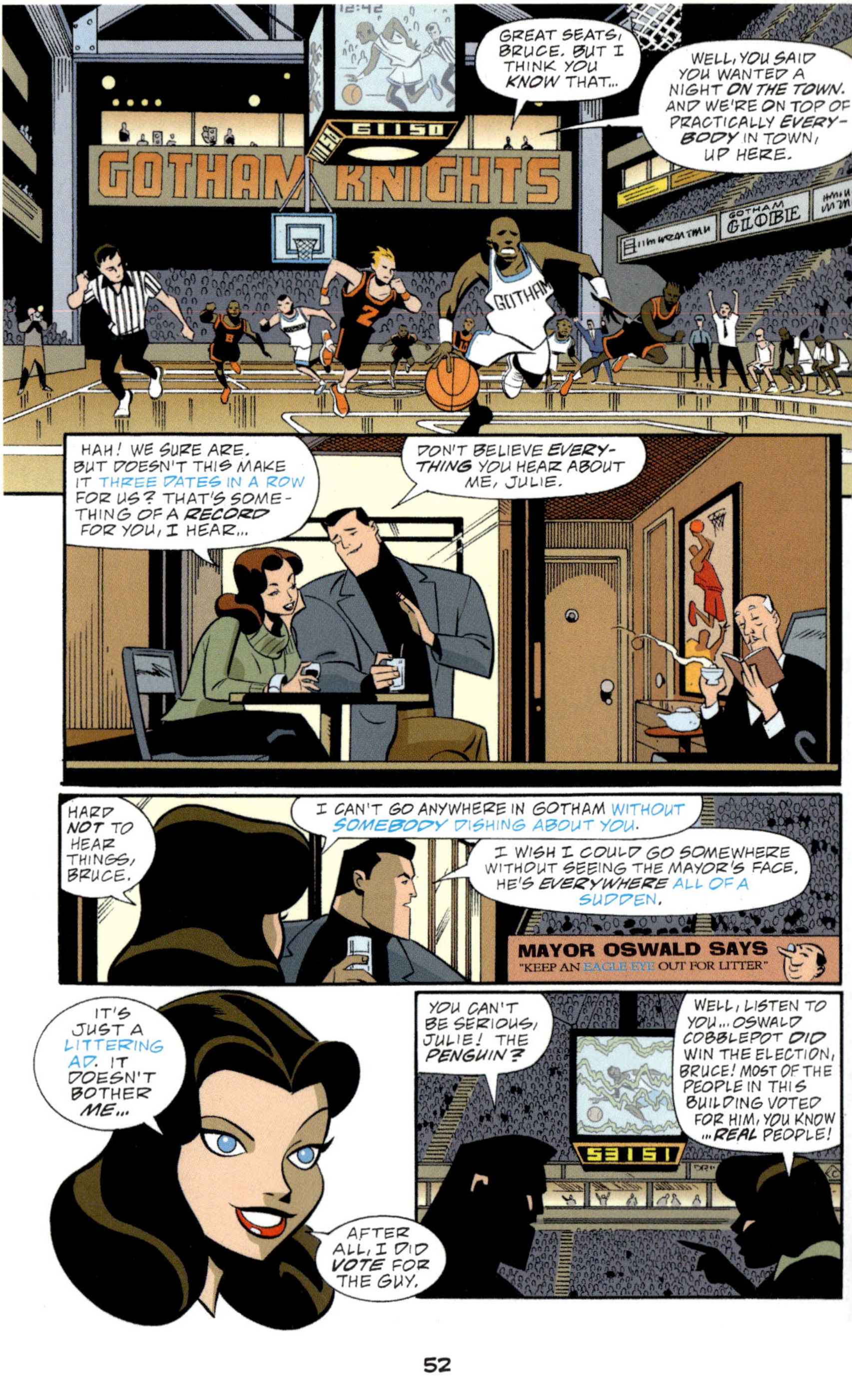
GOTHAM KNIGHTS
GOTHAM GLOBE
GREAT SEATS, BRUCE. BUT I THINK YOU KNOW THAT...
WELL, YOU SAID YOU WANTED A NIGHT ON THE TOWN. AND WE'RE ON TOP OF PRACTICALLY EVERY-BODY IN TOWN, UP HERE.
HAH! WE SURE ARE. BUT DOESN'T THIS MAKE IT THREE DATES IN A ROW FOR US? THAT'S SOME-THING OF A RECORD FOR YOU, I HEAR...
DON'T BELIEVE EVERY-THING YOU HEAR ABOUT ME, JULIE.
HARD NOT TO HEAR THINGS, BRUCE.
I CAN'T GO ANYWHERE IN GOTHAM WITHOUT SOMEBODY DISHING ABOUT YOU.
I WISH I COULD GO SOMEWHERE WITHOUT SEEING THE MAYOR'S FACE. HE'S EVERYWHERE ALL OF A SUDDEN.
MAYOR OSWALD SAYS
"KEEP AN EAGLE EYE OUT FOR LITTER"
IT'S JUST A LITTERING AD. IT DOESN'T BOTHER ME...
AFTER ALL, I DID VOTE FOR THE GUY.
YOU CAN'T BE SERIOUS, JULIE! THE PENGUIN?
WELL, LISTEN TO YOU... OSWALD COBBLEPOT DID WIN THE ELECTION, BRUCE! MOST OF THE PEOPLE IN THIS BUILDING VOTED FOR HIM, YOU KNOW ...REAL PEOPLE!

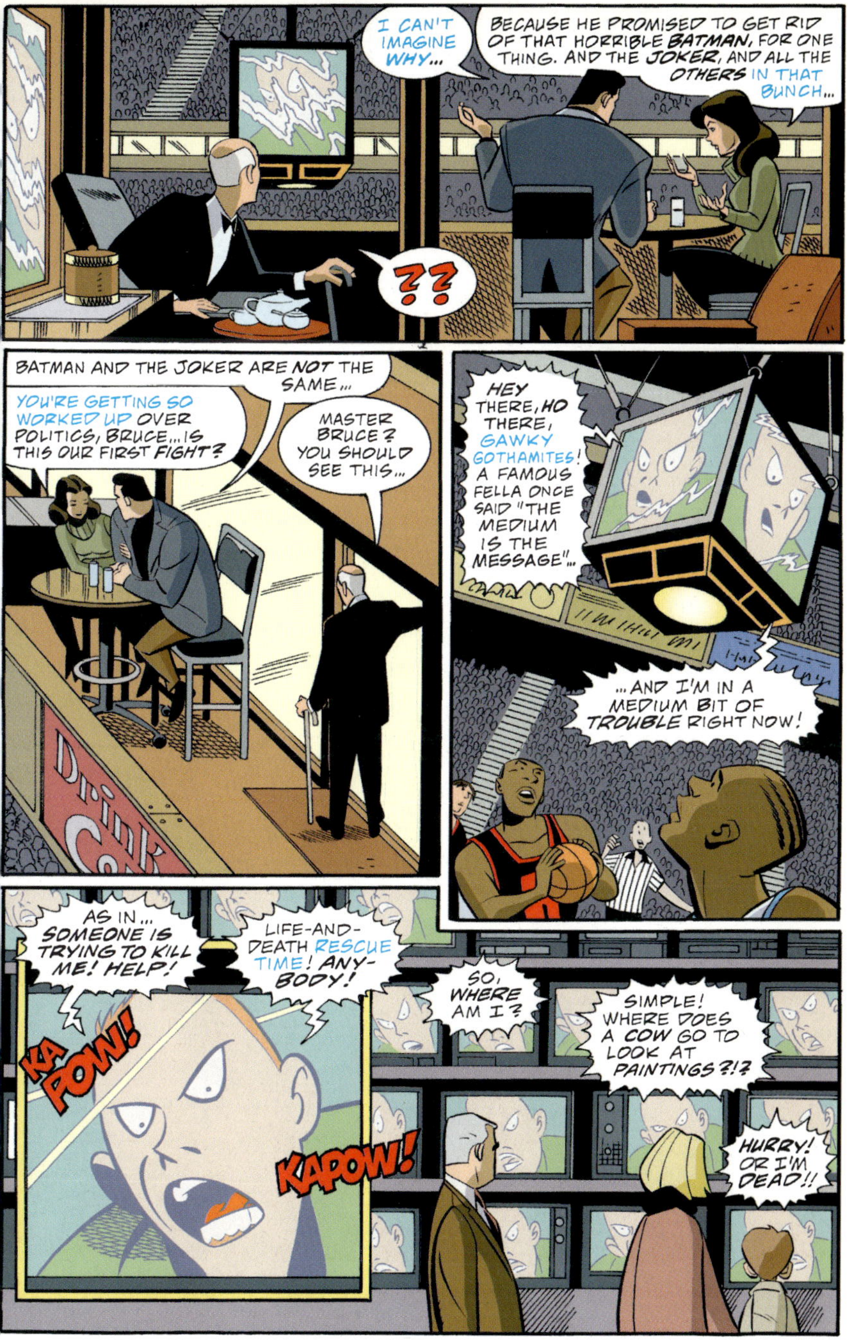
I CAN'T IMAGINE WHY...
BECAUSE HE PROMISED TO GET RID OF THAT HORRIBLE BATMAN, FOR ONE THING. AND THE JOKER, AND ALL THE OTHERS IN THAT BUNCH...
??
BATMAN AND THE JOKER ARE NOT THE SAME...
YOU'RE GETTING SO WORKED UP OVER POLITICS, BRUCE... IS THIS OUR FIRST FIGHT?
MASTER BRUCE? YOU SHOULD SEE THIS...
Drink Coke
HEY THERE, HO THERE, GAWKY GOTHAMITES! A FAMOUS FELLA ONCE SAID "THE MEDIUM IS THE MESSAGE"...
...AND I'M IN A MEDIUM BIT OF TROUBLE RIGHT NOW!
AS IN... SOMEONE IS TRYING TO KILL ME! HELP!
LIFE-AND-DEATH RESCUE TIME! ANYBODY!
KA POW!
KAPOW!
SO, WHERE AM I?
SIMPLE! WHERE DOES A COW GO TO LOOK AT PAINTINGS?!?
HURRY! OR I'M DEAD!!

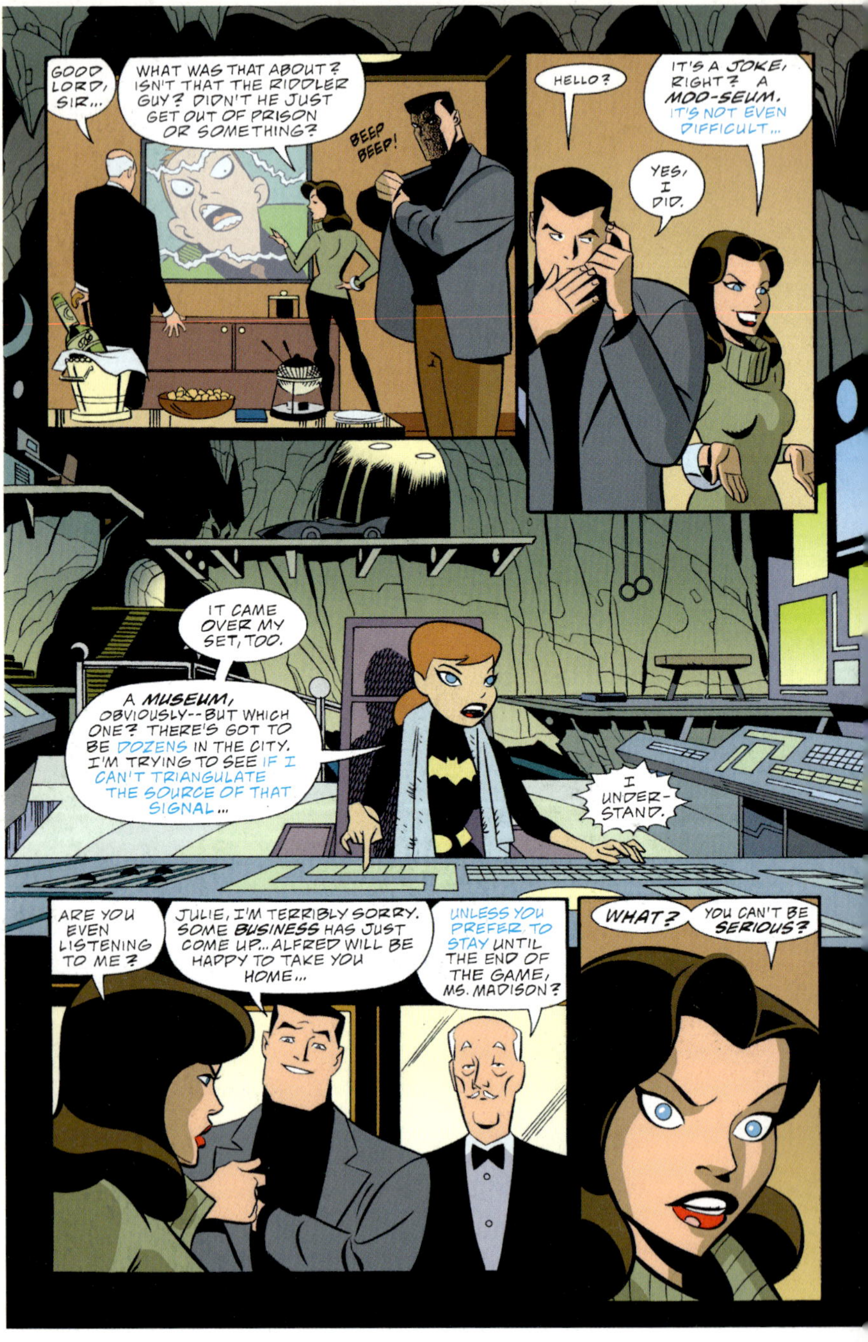
GOOD LORD, SIR...
WHAT WAS THAT ABOUT? ISN'T THAT THE RIDDLER GUY? DIDN'T HE JUST GET OUT OF PRISON OR SOMETHING?
BEEP BEEP!
HELLO?
IT'S A JOKE, RIGHT? A MOO-SEUM. IT'S NOT EVEN DIFFICULT...
YES, I DID.
IT CAME OVER MY SET, TOO.
A MUSEUM, OBVIOUSLY--BUT WHICH ONE? THERE'S GOT TO BE DOZENS IN THE CITY. I'M TRYING TO SEE IF I CAN'T TRIANGULATE THE SOURCE OF THAT SIGNAL...
I UNDER-STAND.
ARE YOU EVEN LISTENING TO ME?
JULIE, I'M TERRIBLY SORRY. SOME BUSINESS HAS JUST COME UP... ALFRED WILL BE HAPPY TO TAKE YOU HOME...
UNLESS YOU PREFER TO STAY UNTIL THE END OF THE GAME, MS. MADISON?
WHAT?
YOU CAN'T BE SERIOUS?

KPOW! KPOW!
KPOW! KPOW!
AAAHH!
HOW DO YOU FLY THIS THING?!?
MUSEUM OF BROADCAST HISTORY
KRASH!
YOUR LUCKY DAY
SMOKIN' GUNS
OOGH... WHO ARE YOU GUYS?!?
WHAT DID I EVER DO TO YOU?
NO MORE QUESTIONS, EDWARD.
DON'T I GET ANY ANSWERS? WHO SENT YOU? WHAT'S GOING ON HERE?!?
YOU HAVE QUESTIONS? SO DO WE...
GOD, BUDDHA, OR ZEUS?
PICK ONE--AND START PRAYING.

THWOK!
SLAM!
KPOW!
WHAM!
GUESS I PICKED THE RIGHT ONE...
VIP!
KPOW!
HOLY COW! BATMAN?!?
FREEZE!
YOUR LUCKY D

SMOKIN' GUNS
NOW YOU'VE GOT ME IN A CROSSFIRE?!
WHAT KIND OF RESCUE IS THIS?!?
YOUR LUCKY DAY
SHUT UP, EDDIE!
POW!
KPOW
THAT'S MORE LIKE IT... THE OTHER ONE'S LEAVING.
NOT IF I CAN HELP IT!
KPOW!
WHAM!

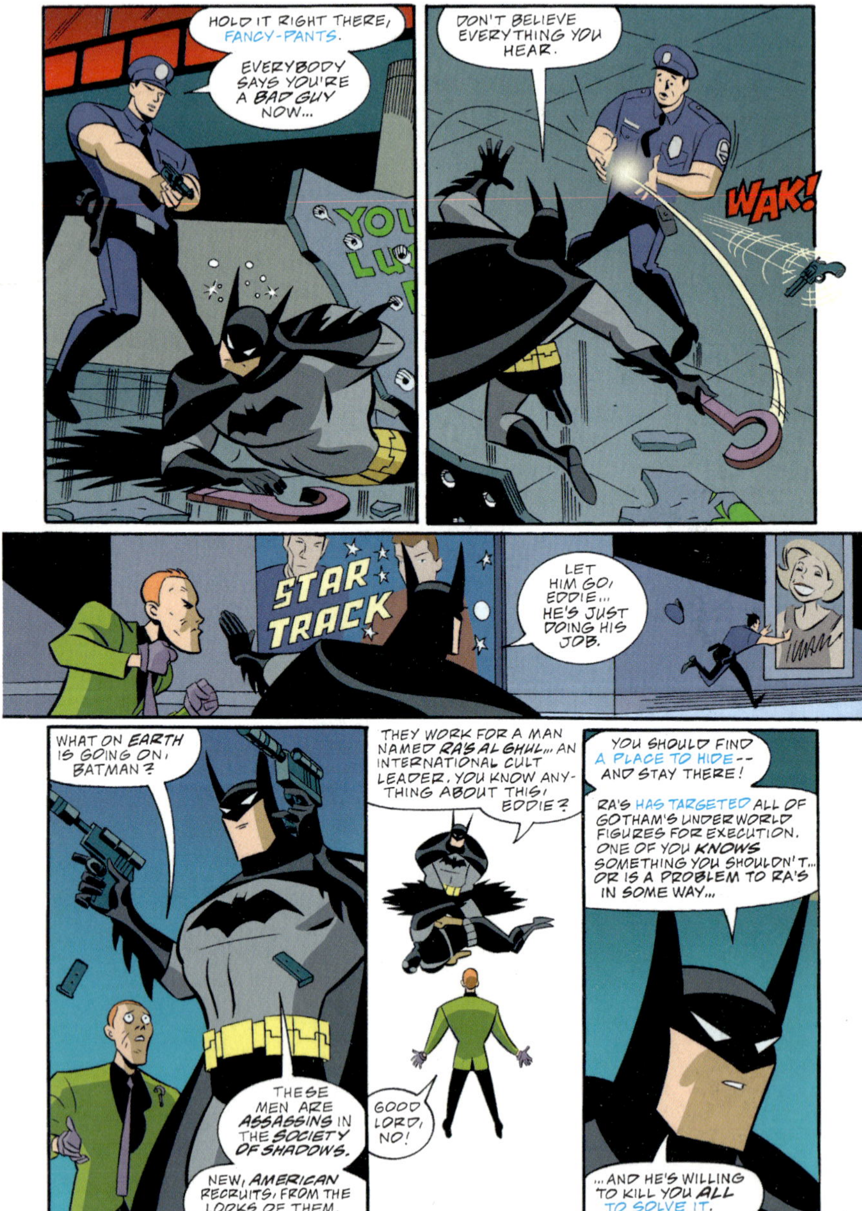
HOLD IT RIGHT THERE, FANCY-PANTS.
EVERYBODY SAYS YOU'RE A BAD GUY NOW...
DON'T BELIEVE EVERYTHING YOU HEAR.
WAK!
STAR TRACK
LET HIM GO, EDDIE... HE'S JUST DOING HIS JOB.
WHAT ON EARTH IS GOING ON, BATMAN?
THESE MEN ARE ASSASSINS IN THE SOCIETY OF SHADOWS.
NEW, AMERICAN RECRUITS, FROM THE LOOKS OF THEM.
THEY WORK FOR A MAN NAMED RA'S AL GHUL... AN INTERNATIONAL CULT LEADER. YOU KNOW ANYTHING ABOUT THIS, EDDIE?
GOOD LORD, NO!
YOU SHOULD FIND A PLACE TO HIDE-- AND STAY THERE!
RA'S HAS TARGETED ALL OF GOTHAM'S UNDERWORLD FIGURES FOR EXECUTION. ONE OF YOU KNOWS SOMETHING YOU SHOULDN'T... OR IS A PROBLEM TO RA'S IN SOME WAY...
...AND HE'S WILLING TO KILL YOU ALL TO SOLVE IT.

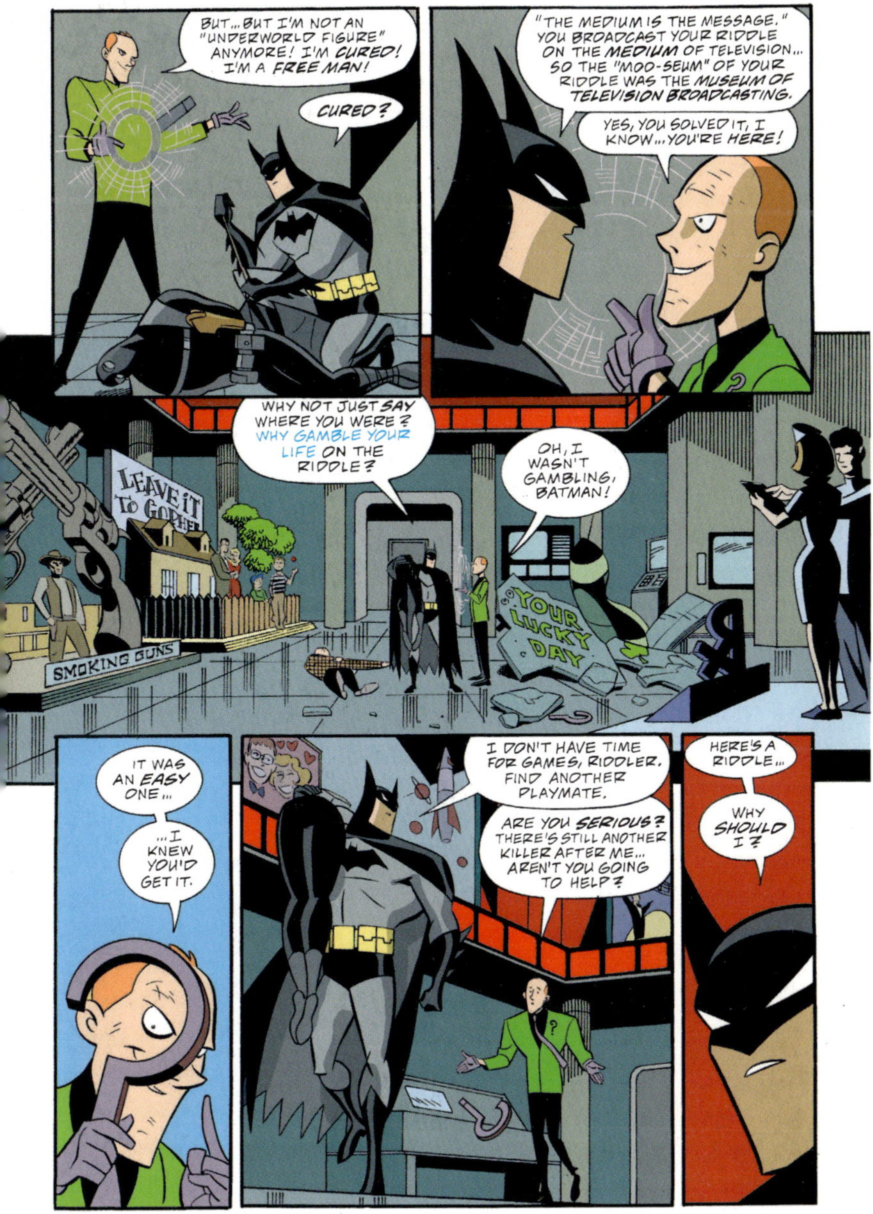
BUT... BUT I'M NOT AN "UNDERWORLD FIGURE" ANYMORE! I'M CURED! I'M A FREE MAN!
CURED?
"THE MEDIUM IS THE MESSAGE." YOU BROADCAST YOUR RIDDLE ON THE MEDIUM OF TELEVISION... SO THE "MOO-SEUM" OF YOUR RIDDLE WAS THE MUSEUM OF TELEVISION BROADCASTING.
YES, YOU SOLVED IT, I KNOW... YOU'RE HERE!
WHY NOT JUST SAY WHERE YOU WERE? WHY GAMBLE YOUR LIFE ON THE RIDDLE?
OH, I WASN'T GAMBLING, BATMAN!
LEAVE IT TO GOPHER
SMOKING GUNS
YOUR LUCKY DAY
IT WAS AN EASY ONE...
...I KNEW YOU'D GET IT.
I DON'T HAVE TIME FOR GAMES, RIDDLER. FIND ANOTHER PLAYMATE.
ARE YOU SERIOUS? THERE'S STILL ANOTHER KILLER AFTER ME... AREN'T YOU GOING TO HELP?
HERE'S A RIDDLE...
WHY SHOULD I?

IT IS NOT GOING WELL.
I HAD TO LEAVE BROTHER MARTIN BEHIND.
THAT IS, INDEED, NOT GOING WELL.
I HAVE ALSO LOST DIRECT CONTACT WITH MY TARGET...
HOW?
WE ENCOUNTERED BATMAN. HE INCAPACITATED MY PARTNER BEFORE EITHER OF US COULD WITHDRAW.
THE PRIME ORDER IS CLEAR. YOU ARE NOT TO ENGAGE THE DETECTIVE. WE MUST MOVE ON TO ANOTHER TARGET.
BUT I CAN FINISH THIS ASSIGNMENT, MASTER.
NO. YOU HAVE LOST THE-- SQUAWK!!
HEY THERE, MEDIA WATCHERS!
PLEASE ACCEPT A PERSONAL APOLOGY TO EVERY TOM, DICK, HARRY, CLIFFORD, IRVING AND EMILE OUT THERE FOR INTERRUPTING TV AGAIN, BUT IT IS A LIFE-AND-DEATH THING --
--AND I DON'T HAPPEN TO HAVE BATMAN'S HOME PHONE...

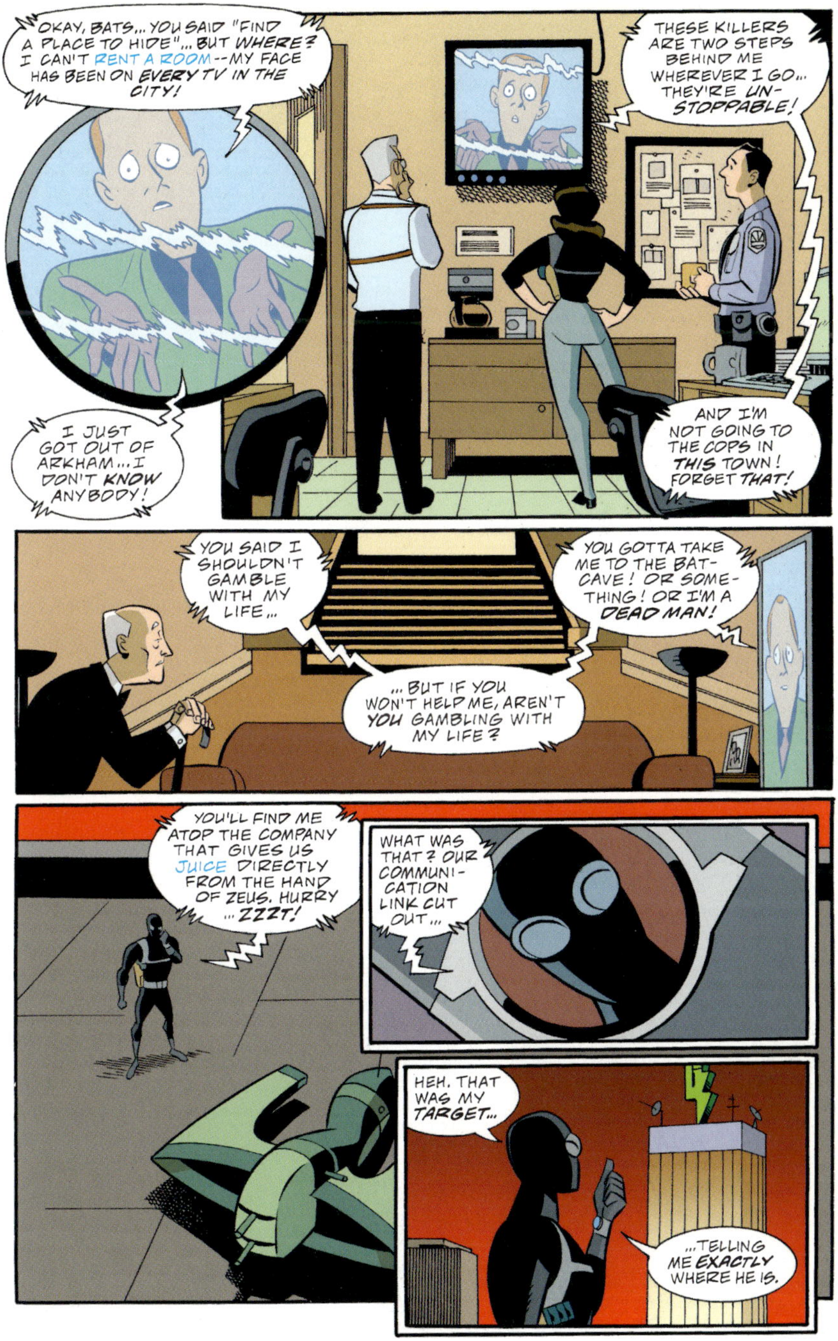
OKAY, BATS... YOU SAID "FIND A PLACE TO HIDE"... BUT WHERE? I CAN'T RENT A ROOM--MY FACE HAS BEEN ON EVERY TV IN THE CITY!
I JUST GOT OUT OF ARKHAM... I DON'T KNOW ANYBODY!
THESE KILLERS ARE TWO STEPS BEHIND ME WHEREVER I GO... THEY'RE UN-STOPPABLE!
AND I'M NOT GOING TO THE COPS IN THIS TOWN! FORGET THAT!
YOU SAID I SHOULDN'T GAMBLE WITH MY LIFE...
...BUT IF YOU WON'T HELP ME, AREN'T YOU GAMBLING WITH MY LIFE?
YOU GOTTA TAKE ME TO THE BAT-CAVE! OR SOME-THING! OR I'M A DEAD MAN!
YOU'LL FIND ME ATOP THE COMPANY THAT GIVES US JUICE DIRECTLY FROM THE HAND OF ZEUS. HURRY ...ZZZT!
WHAT WAS THAT? OUR COMMUNI-CATION LINK CUT OUT...
HEH. THAT WAS MY TARGET...
...TELLING ME EXACTLY WHERE HE IS.

ZEUS CONTROLLED THE LIGHTNING-- ANY SCHOOL-CHILD KNOWS THAT!
THE LIGHTNING LOGO ON THE POWER TOWER HAS BEEN A GOTHAM LAND-MARK FOR YEARS...
YOU MUST THINK I'M A COMPLETE IDIOT!
KPOW! KPOW KPOW KPOW!
YEAH, AN IDIOT...MORE OR LESS.

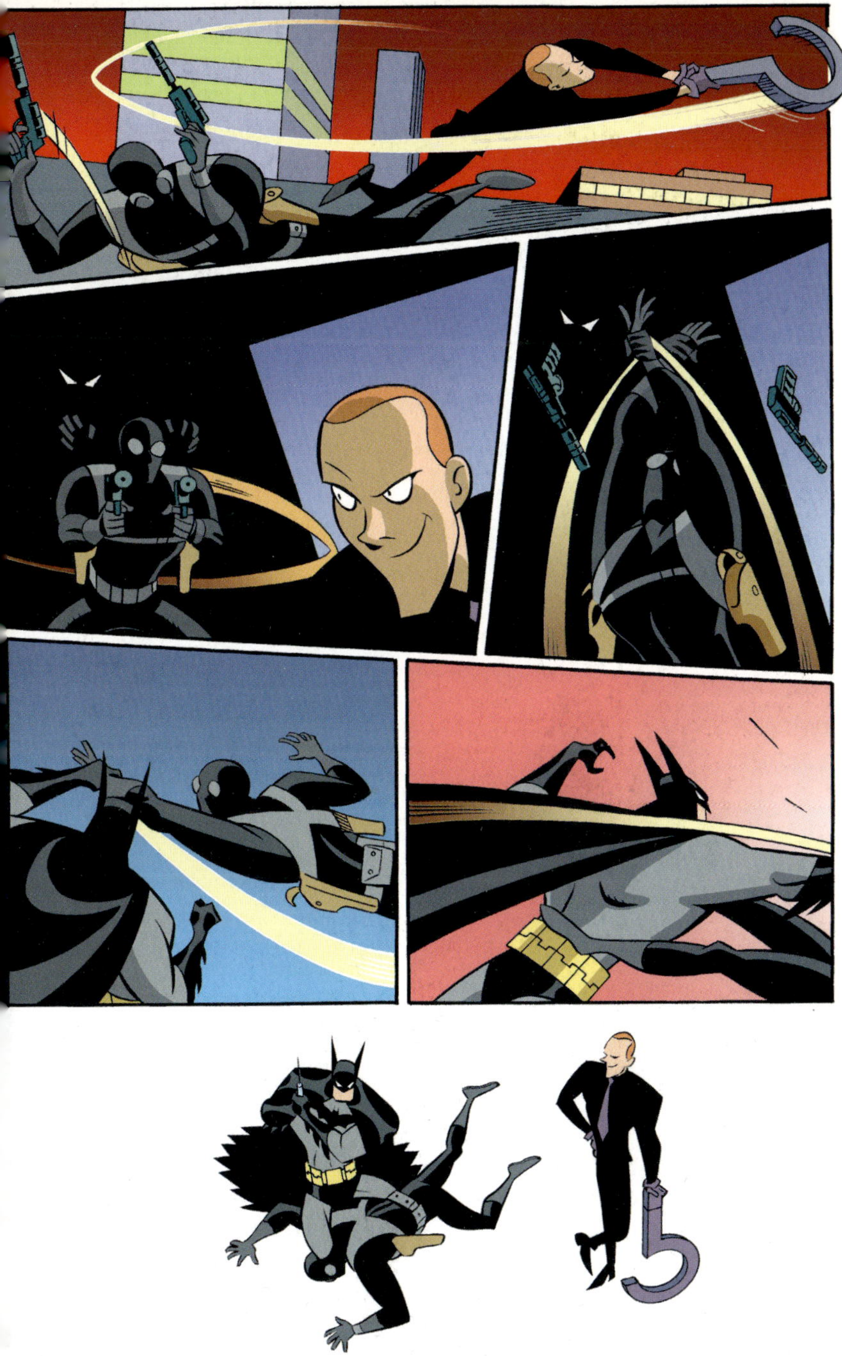

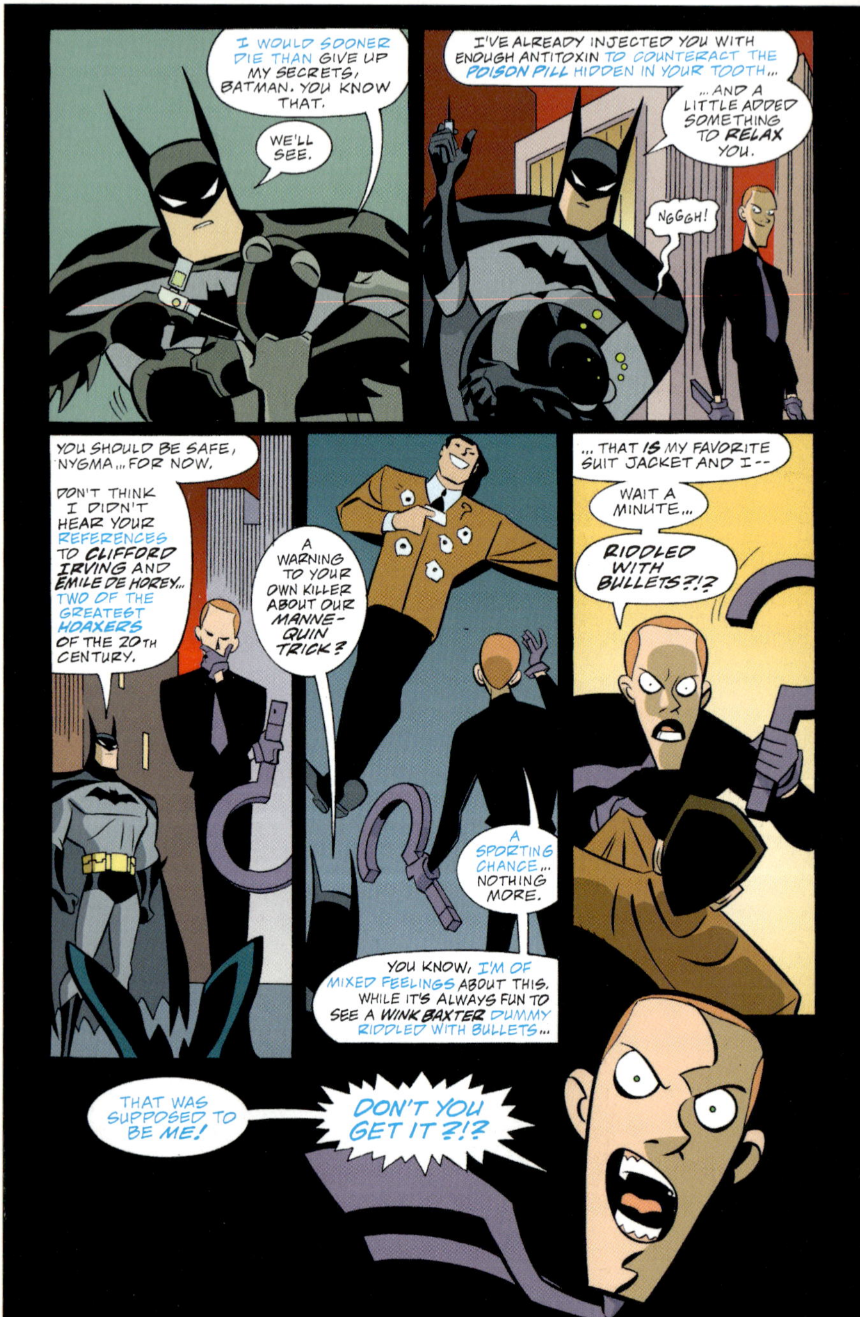
I WOULD SOONER DIE THAN GIVE UP MY SECRETS, BATMAN. YOU KNOW THAT.
WE'LL SEE.
I'VE ALREADY INJECTED YOU WITH ENOUGH ANTITOXIN TO COUNTERACT THE POISON PILL HIDDEN IN YOUR TOOTH...
...AND A LITTLE ADDED SOMETHING TO RELAX YOU.
NGGGH!
YOU SHOULD BE SAFE, NYGMA... FOR NOW.
DON'T THINK I DIDN'T HEAR YOUR REFERENCES TO CLIFFORD IRVING AND EMILE DE HOREY... TWO OF THE GREATEST HOAXERS OF THE 20TH CENTURY.
A WARNING TO YOUR OWN KILLER ABOUT OUR MANNEQUIN TRICK?
A SPORTING CHANCE... NOTHING MORE.
YOU KNOW, I'M OF MIXED FEELINGS ABOUT THIS. WHILE IT'S ALWAYS FUN TO SEE A WINK BAXTER DUMMY RIDDLED WITH BULLETS...
...THAT IS MY FAVORITE SUIT JACKET AND I--
WAIT A MINUTE...
RIDDLED WITH BULLETS?!?
THAT WAS SUPPOSED TO BE ME!
DON'T YOU GET IT?!?

THAT WOULD HAVE BEEN THE ULTIMATE EXIT FOR ME! WHAT HAPPENS TO ME NOW?
I SLIP IN THE BATHTUB, OR GET HIT BY A BUS SOMEDAY?!?
WHEN AM I GOING TO GET THIS KIND OF CHANCE AGAIN?
RIDDLED BY BULLETS!
IT WOULD HAVE BEEN PERFECT ...AND YOU RUINED IT!
YOU'RE SICK, RIDDLER.
YOU SHOULDN'T BE OUT. YOU'RE NOT READY.
YOU MAY HAVE FOOLED THE DOCTORS AND THE LAWYERS, BUT I KNOW THE TRUTH.
YOU MAY BE WALKING AROUND OUTSIDE THE BARS RIGHT NOW...
...BUT YOU'RE NOT A FREE MAN.

future site of MAMMOTH STUDIOS
GRAY GHOST
WAUGH-WA-WA.
IT SEEMS ONLY FITTING THAT A GROUND-BREAKING MAYOR LIKE MYSELF...
...IS BREAKING GROUND AT THE SITE OF THIS NEW VENTURE!
THANKS TO MY TIRELESS EFFORTS, MAMMOTH STUDIOS WILL BE SETTING UP SHOP IN OUR FAIR CITY!
SOME POLITICOS MAY PROMISE YOU THE STARS, BUT OSWALD C. COBBLEPOT DELIVERS!
WELCOMES THE future site of MAMMOTH STUDIOS
MY DEAR CONSTITUENTS...
...THIS WON'T JUST BRING BUSINESS AND TOURISM TO GOTHAM. IT WILL ALSO BRING...
CLAP CLAP CLAP CLAP CLAP!
...A TOUCH OF CLASS!
SLOTT--WRITER
TEMPLETON--PENCILLER
BEATTY--INKER
ZYLONOL--COLORIST
FELIX--LETTERER
RICHARDS--ASSISTANT
HILTY--EDITOR
BATMAN CREATED BY BOB KANE
FOWL PLAY

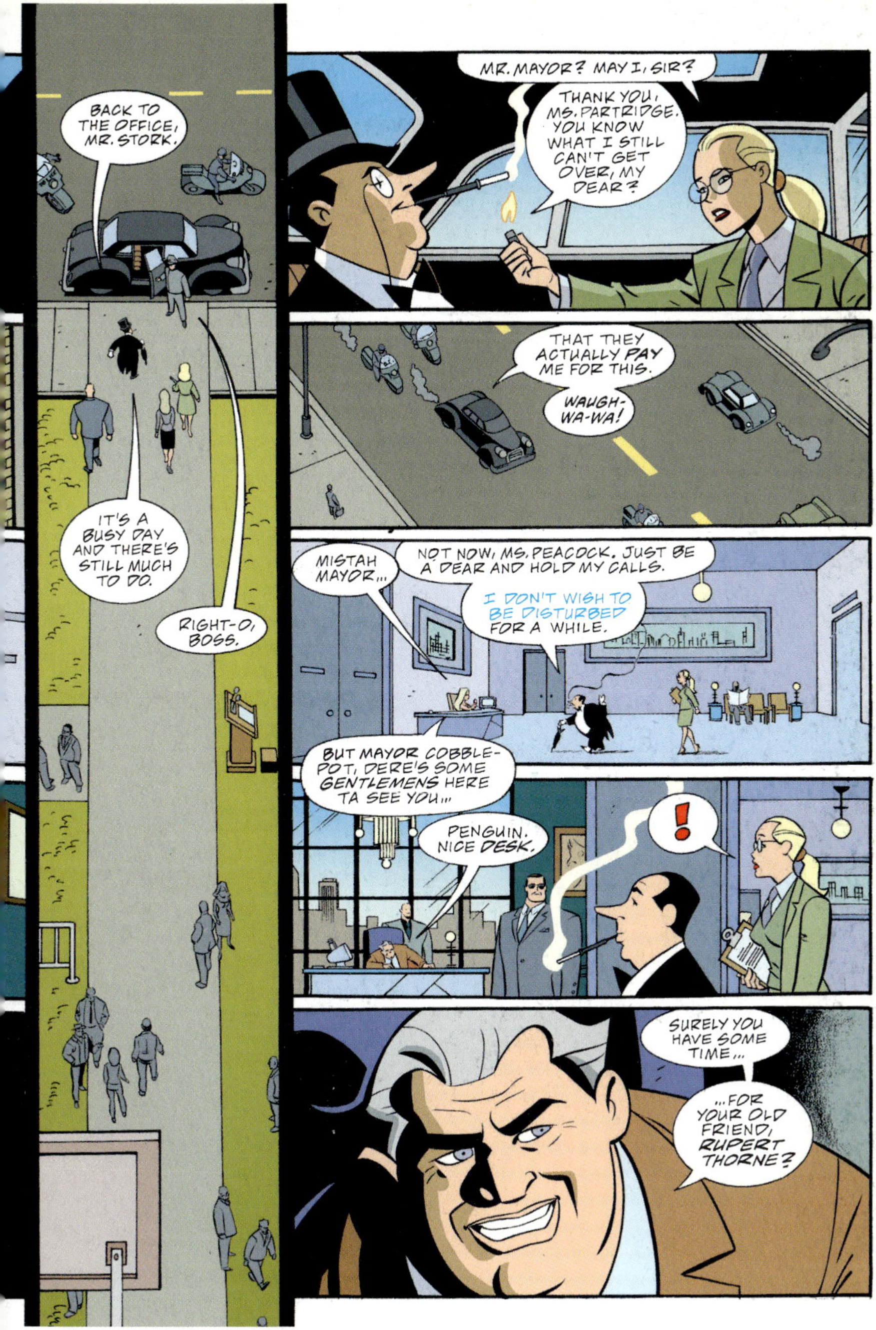
BACK TO THE OFFICE, MR. STORK.
IT'S A BUSY DAY AND THERE'S STILL MUCH TO DO.
RIGHT-O, BOSS.
MR. MAYOR? MAY I, SIR?
THANK YOU, MS. PARTRIDGE. YOU KNOW WHAT I STILL CAN'T GET OVER, MY DEAR?
THAT THEY ACTUALLY PAY ME FOR THIS.
WAUGH-WA-WA!
MISTAH MAYOR...
NOT NOW, MS. PEACOCK. JUST BE A DEAR AND HOLD MY CALLS.
I DON'T WISH TO BE DISTURBED FOR A WHILE.
BUT MAYOR COBBLE-POT, DERE'S SOME GENTLEMENS HERE TA SEE YOU...
PENGUIN. NICE DESK.
!
SURELY YOU HAVE SOME TIME...
...FOR YOUR OLD FRIEND, RUPERT THORNE?

AH, YES, NOT TO FEAR; I'VE BEEN EXPECTING THESE... FELLOWS.
MS. PARTRIDGE, IF YOU'D EXCUSE US.
YES, SIR.
RUPERT, WE'RE BOTH BUSY MEN.
WHAT SAY WE SKIP THE CHITCHAT AND TALK TURKEY?
ACTUALLY, PENGUIN, I'M HERE TO TALK GRAVY.
A NEW MOVIE STUDIO'S COMING TO GOTHAM. THAT'S GOING TO MEAN A LOT OF CONSTRUCTION WORK.
SOMEONE WITH THE RIGHT CONNECTIONS TO THE ZONING BOARD COULD REALLY CLEAN UP.
SO I THOUGHT I'D PRESENT YOU WITH FOUR MILLION REASONS...
...THAT "SOMEONE" SHOULD BE ME.
LET ME GET THIS STRAIGHT...
YOU FEATHER MY NEST, AND I MAKE SURE THE CONTRACT GOES TO YOUR CONSTRUCTION COMPANY.
HA! YOU ALWAYS WERE A BLUNT OLD BIRD!
YES. DO WE HAVE A DEAL?
OF COURSE, RUPERT. OF COURSE.

I TRUST YOU GOT ALL THAT?
YES, SIR.
FREEZE! GOTHAM POLICE! YOU'RE ALL UNDER ARREST!
MAYOR COBBLEPOT IS NOT FOR SALE, THORNE. MY WHOLE LIFE, ALL I'VE EVER CRAVED WAS POWER AND RESPECT.
MONEY? WHAT CAN MONEY GET ME THAT I DON'T ALREADY HAVE?!
KRASH!
MR. MAYOR! BEHIND YOU! ONE OF THEM IS GETTING AWAY!
MADRE DE DIOS!
GOTHAM CITY HALL

OH, LET HIM GO.
WE'VE GOT THE BIG FISH. GOOD WORK, DETECTIVE MACAW.
THAT'S MONTOYA, SIR.
WHATEVER. WAUGH-WA-WA.
YOU CAN STOP RECORDING. WE DIDN'T GET ANYTHING I CAN USE.
VERY WELL. MAYBE NEXT TIME, MASTER BRUCE.
NOT "MAYBE", ALFRED.
THE PENGUIN WILL SLIP UP.
AND WHEN HE DOES--I WILL BE THERE.
WHEN GOTHAM SPEAKS, HE LISTENS! MAYOR COBBLEPOT CARES.
THE END

Vokabelerklärungen (S. 72–81)

S. 72/73
evil [ˈihvəl] böse
Knievel [ˈnihvəl] *amerikanischer Motorrad-Stuntman*
honey-bun [ˈhaniban] Süße
vat [vät] Bottich
raisins [ˈräisəns] Rosinen
I s'pose (= suppose) [ai ßpous] nehme ich an
the mayhem [ðə ˈmäihem] das Chaos
the destruction [ðə diˈßtrakschən] die Zerstörung
Perish the thought. [ˈperisch ðə θaht] Gott bewahre!
I had them delivered. [ai häd ðəm diˈlivərd] Ich habe sie liefern lassen.
I was gonna (= going to) dive-bomb city hall [ai wəs ˈgəna ˈdaivbahm ˈßiti hahl] ich hatte vor, das Rathaus im Sturzflug zu bombardieren
from a sticky motorbike [frəm ə ˈßtiki ˈmoutərbaik] von einem klebrigen Motorrad aus
you're not yourself anymore [jur naht jurˈßelf eniˈmohr] du bist nicht mehr du selbst
those head-shrinking creeps [ðous ˈhedschrinking krihpß] diese kopfschrumpfenden Widerlinge

S. 74/75
Snap out of it! [ßnäp aut əv it] Komm wieder zu dir!
ya (= you) sickening love puppy [jə ˈßikəning lav ˈpapi] du widerliches verliebtes Hündchen
mortars [ˈmohrtərs] Minenwerfer
to advertise [tə ˈädvərtais] zu inserieren
beat-up [ˈbihtap] zerbeult
collectors [kəˈlektərs] Sammler

S. 76/77
a wanted man [ə ˈwahntid män] ein polizeilich gesuchter Mann
inmates [ˈinmäitß] Insassen
we're still assessing the situation [wir ßtil əˈßeßing ðə ßitschuˈäischən] wir sind noch dabei, die Situation einzuschätzen
we can only consider it fortunate [wi kən ˈounli kənˈßidər it ˈfohrtschənət] wir können es nur als glücklichen Umstand betrachten
his blindfold [his ˈblaindfould] seine Augenbinde
my buddies [mai ˈbadis] meine Freunde/Kumpel
vengeance [ˈvendschənß] Rache

S. 78/79
survival instinct [ßərˈvaivəl ˈinßtinkt] Überlebensinstinkt
your natural inclination for [jur ˈnätschərəl inkləˈnäischən fər] dein natürlicher Hang zu
cheating [ˈtschihting] Mogelei

S. 80/81
your physical prowess [jur ˈfisikəl ˈprauəß] deine körperlichen Fähigkeiten

▶ *Nächste Ausklappseite: S. 91*

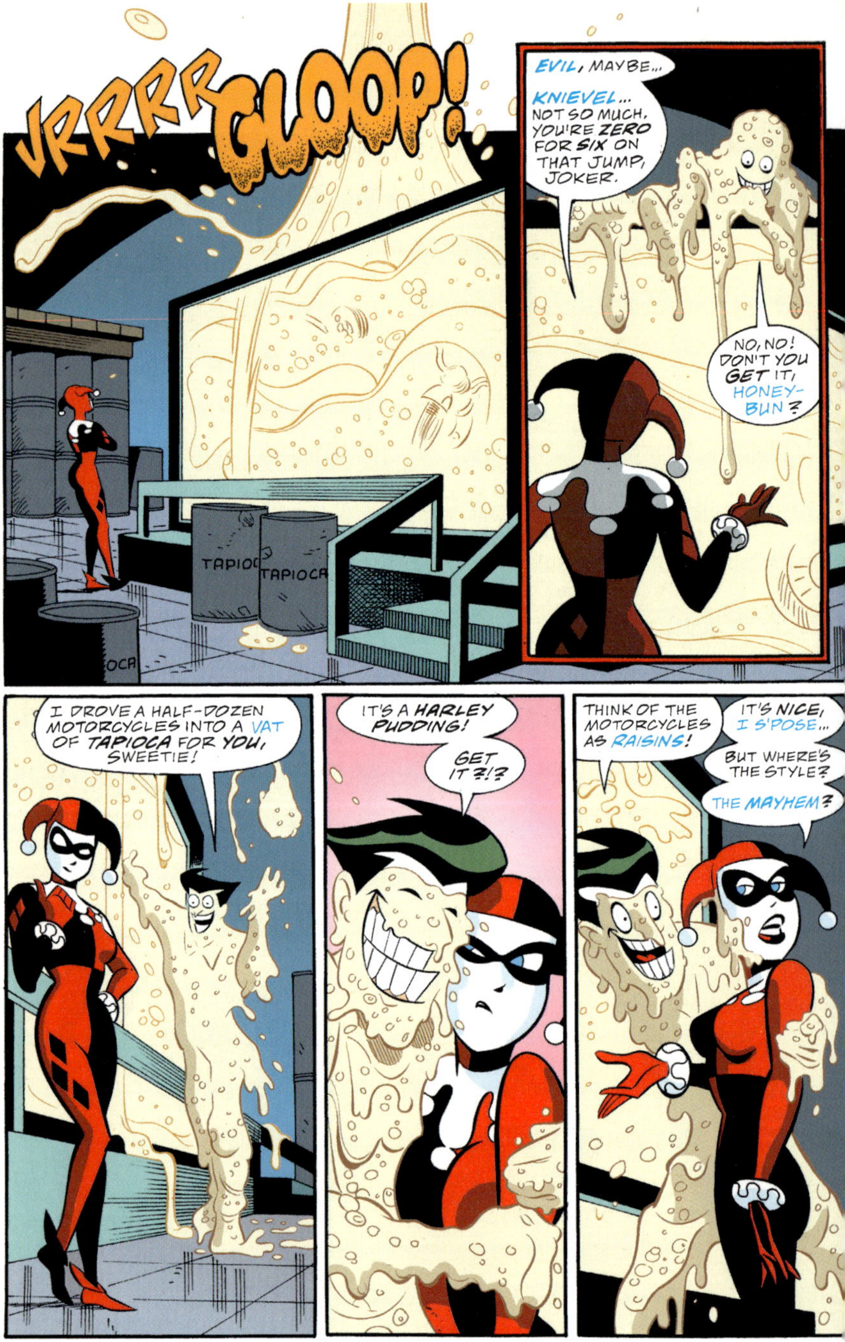
VRRRR GLOOP!
EVIL, MAYBE...
KNIEVEL... NOT SO MUCH. YOU'RE ZERO FOR SIX ON THAT JUMP, JOKER.
NO, NO! DON'T YOU GET IT, HONEY-BUN?
I DROVE A HALF-DOZEN MOTORCYCLES INTO A VAT OF TAPIOCA FOR YOU, SWEETIE!
IT'S A HARLEY PUDDING!
GET IT?!?
THINK OF THE MOTORCYCLES AS RAISINS!
IT'S NICE, I S'POSE...
BUT WHERE'S THE STYLE?
THE MAYHEM?
TAPIOCA
TAPIOCA

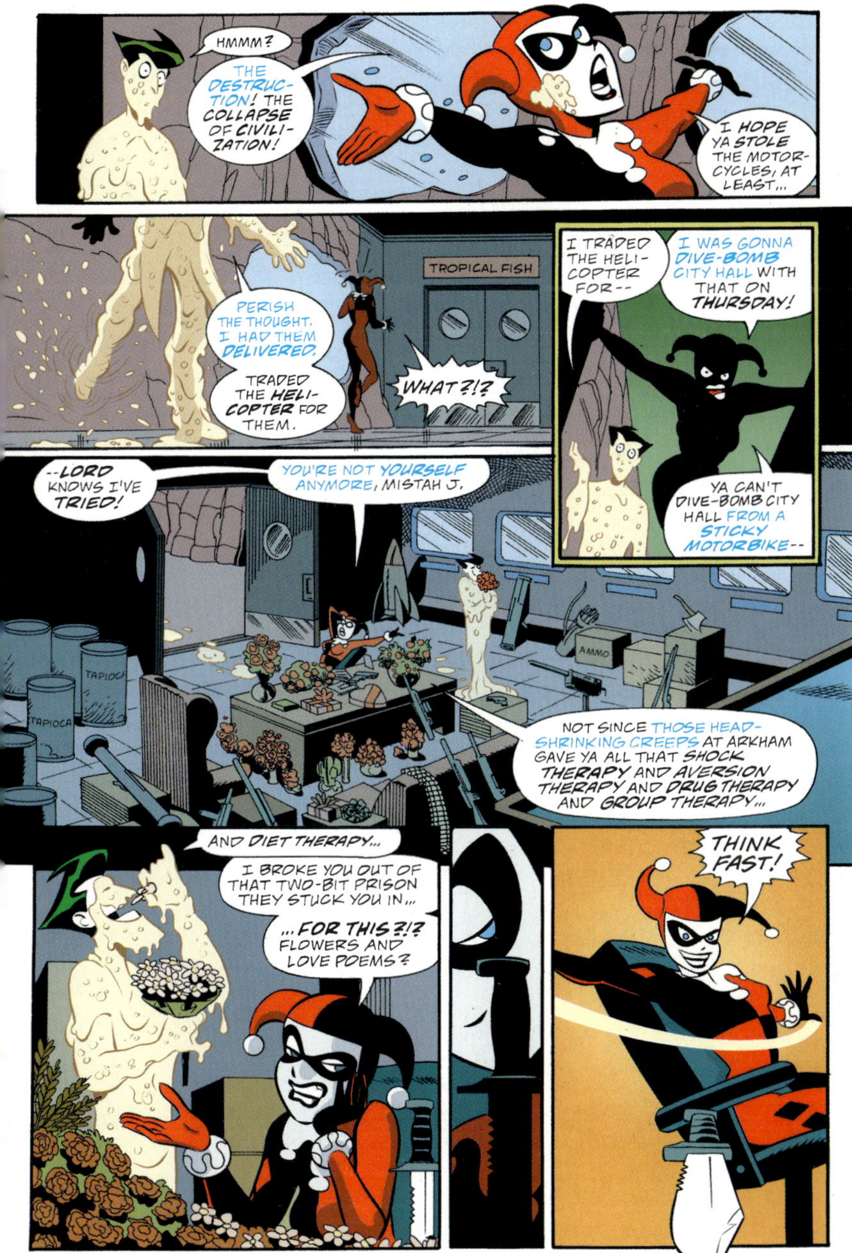
HMMM?
THE DESTRUCTION! THE COLLAPSE OF CIVILIZATION!
I HOPE YA STOLE THE MOTORCYCLES, AT LEAST...
PERISH THE THOUGHT. I HAD THEM DELIVERED.
TRADED THE HELICOPTER FOR THEM.
TROPICAL FISH
WHAT?!?
I TRADED THE HELICOPTER FOR--
I WAS GONNA DIVE-BOMB CITY HALL WITH THAT ON THURSDAY!
YA CAN'T DIVE-BOMB CITY HALL FROM A STICKY MOTORBIKE--
--LORD KNOWS I'VE TRIED!
YOU'RE NOT YOURSELF ANYMORE, MISTAH J.
TAPIOCA
TAPIOCA
AMMO
NOT SINCE THOSE HEAD-SHRINKING CREEPS AT ARKHAM GAVE YA ALL THAT SHOCK THERAPY AND AVERSION THERAPY AND DRUG THERAPY AND GROUP THERAPY...
AND DIET THERAPY...
I BROKE YOU OUT OF THAT TWO-BIT PRISON THEY STUCK YOU IN...
...FOR THIS?!? FLOWERS AND LOVE POEMS?
THINK FAST!

THUK!
HMMM?
SNAP OUT OF IT!
I JUST TRIED TO KILL YOU, AND YOU DIDN'T EVEN BLINK!
AWWW-- YOU COULD NEVER HURT ME, BABY...
YOU LOVE ME TOO MUCH!
COME, LET'S TANGO!
NAH...
YOU'RE RIGHT. IT'S NOT IN ME.
I COULDN'T KILL YA...
...BUT I KNOW SOMEONE WHO COULD.
HEY, YA SICKENING LOVE PUPPY... WANNA GO ON A ROAD TRIP?
WITH YOU?
YOU BET!
GET THE MORTARS!
GOTHAM GLOBE
SHADOW ASSASSIN CAUGHT IN ARKHAM ATTACK
SEE PG. 3 FOR STORY

PINKY'S USED CARS
TAPPA TAPPA TAP TAP
PINKY McCONNEL?
AHH!
BATMAN!
BAD ENOUGH THAT YOU DO BUSINESS WITH A CRIMINAL MADMAN LIKE THE JOKER...
...BUT TO ADVERTISE "THE JOKER'S HELICOPTER" FOR SALE ON E-BUY... THAT'S JUST STUPID.
DO YOU KNOW WHAT IT'S WORTH?
IS IT WORTH YOUR LIFE?
LAST YEAR, I SOLD MATT HAGEN'S BEAT-UP OLD BUICK FOR FIFTY THOUSAND DOLLARS! THERE ARE COLLECTORS OUT THERE--
HOW MUCH DID JOKER PAY YOU? WHERE CAN I FIND HIM?

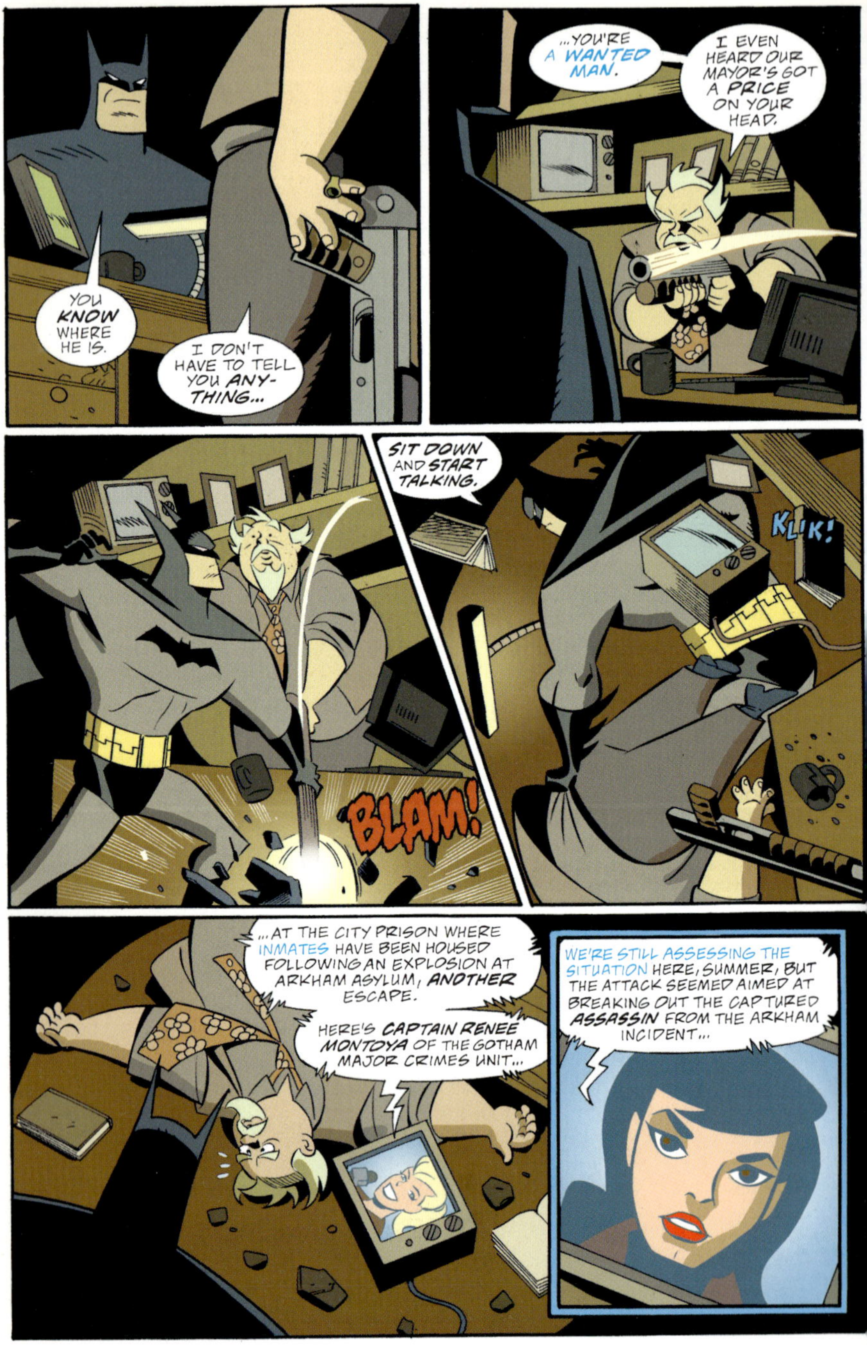
YOU KNOW WHERE HE IS.
I DON'T HAVE TO TELL YOU ANY-THING...
...YOU'RE A WANTED MAN.
I EVEN HEARD OUR MAYOR'S GOT A PRICE ON YOUR HEAD.
BLAM!
SIT DOWN AND START TALKING.
KLIK!
...AT THE CITY PRISON WHERE INMATES HAVE BEEN HOUSED FOLLOWING AN EXPLOSION AT ARKHAM ASYLUM, ANOTHER ESCAPE.
HERE'S CAPTAIN RENEE MONTOYA OF THE GOTHAM MAJOR CRIMES UNIT...
WE'RE STILL ASSESSING THE SITUATION HERE, SUMMER, BUT THE ATTACK SEEMED AIMED AT BREAKING OUT THE CAPTURED ASSASSIN FROM THE ARKHAM INCIDENT...

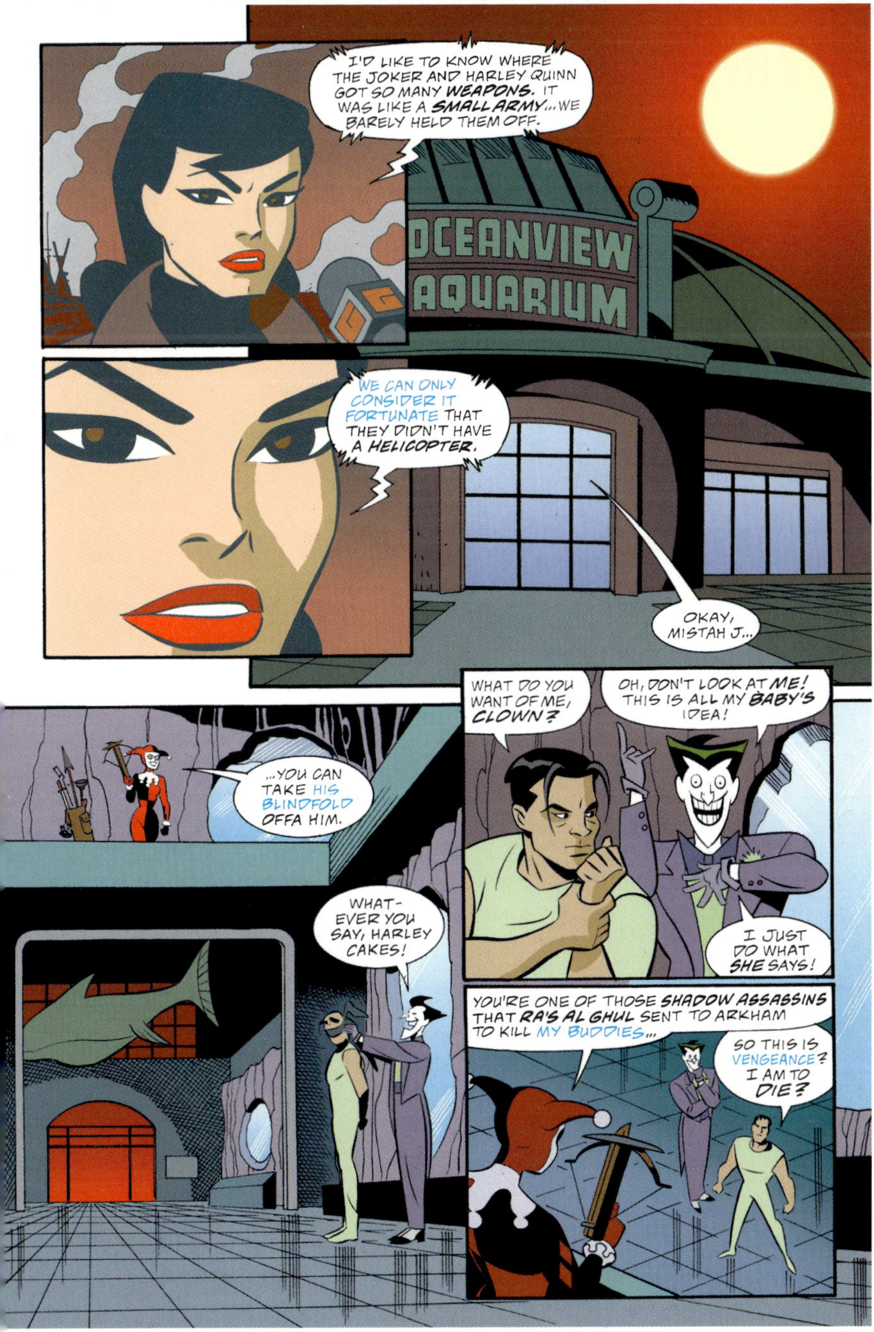

I'D LIKE TO KNOW WHERE THE JOKER AND HARLEY QUINN GOT SO MANY WEAPONS. IT WAS LIKE A SMALL ARMY... WE BARELY HELD THEM OFF.
OCEANVIEW AQUARIUM
WE CAN ONLY CONSIDER IT FORTUNATE THAT THEY DIDN'T HAVE A HELICOPTER.
OKAY, MISTAH J...
...YOU CAN TAKE HIS BLINDFOLD OFFA HIM.
WHAT-EVER YOU SAY, HARLEY CAKES!
WHAT DO YOU WANT OF ME, CLOWN?
OH, DON'T LOOK AT ME! THIS IS ALL MY BABY'S IDEA!
I JUST DO WHAT SHE SAYS!
YOU'RE ONE OF THOSE SHADOW ASSASSINS THAT RA'S AL GHUL SENT TO ARKHAM TO KILL MY BUDDIES...
SO THIS IS VENGEANCE? I AM TO DIE?

HECK NO!
WELLL... PROBABLY NOT, ANYWAY...
I WANT YOU TO FINISH THE JOB--AND TRY TO KILL THE JOKER.
HON...?
DON'T WORRY, BABY... MY MONEY'S ON YOU, NO MATTER WHAT KIND OF KUNG FU WHOOEY-WHAMMY THING HE'S GOT GOING.
THE SURVIVAL INSTINCT IS THE STRONGEST IMPULSE YA GOT. AS SOON AS THE CHIPS ARE DOWN AND YOUR LIFE DEPENDS ON IT...
...YOUR NATURAL INCLINATION FOR CHEATING, HURTING, AND FIGHTING DIRTY WILL SAVE YOU...
...AND I'LL HAVE MY OLD JOKER BACK.
IF NOT--
--I PROMISE I'LL AVENGE YOU AND MOIDER THE BUM!
YOU... YOU'RE DOING THIS ALL FOR ME?
WHAT A GAL!
IF I WAS YOU, MISTAH J... I'D RUN.
EEP!

THERE'S ANOTHER WRECKED VEHICLE...
AND ANOTHER ONE OVER THERE...
JOKER AND HARLEY AREN'T EXACTLY MAKING A DIFFICULT TRAIL TO FOLLOW.
THEY ARE INSANE, YOU KNOW.
HOTEL
IF WE CAN FOLLOW A TRAIL THIS EASILY, SO CAN BATMAN.
THERE'S A GOOD CHANCE HE'LL BECOME INVOLVED IN THIS, COM-MISSIONER.
OUR ORDERS FROM UP TOP ARE TO ARREST HIM ON SIGHT.
ARE YOU READY TO DO THAT?
I'VE BEEN A COP MY WHOLE LIFE, CAPTAIN...
I KNOW MY DUTY.
I'M JUST GOING TO HAVE TO HOPE I DON'T SEE HIM.

WEEEE-HAA!
TAPIOCA
DON'T MAKE THIS DIFFICULT, AND I PROMISE I'LL BE QUICK.
RIGHT...
LIKE, HOW MANY TIMES HAVE I HEARD *THAT?*
PATHETIC...
WHA...?
YANK!

BATMAN!
BUDDY!
THIS IS BETTER THAN A BIRTHDAY!
DETECTIVE!
WHEN LAST YOU FACED ME, AT ARKHAM... YOU DID NOT FACE ME AT ALL.
INSTEAD YOU ATTACKED ME FROM BEHIND.
DO YOU DARE FACE ME NOW-- MAN TO MAN?
THIS SHOULD PROVE INTER-ESTING. I HAVE SUFFERED THROUGH MANY LONG TALES OF YOUR PHYSICAL PROWESS!
BUT I AM MASTER OF FIVE DISCIPLINES.
LET'S PUT IT TO A TEST.

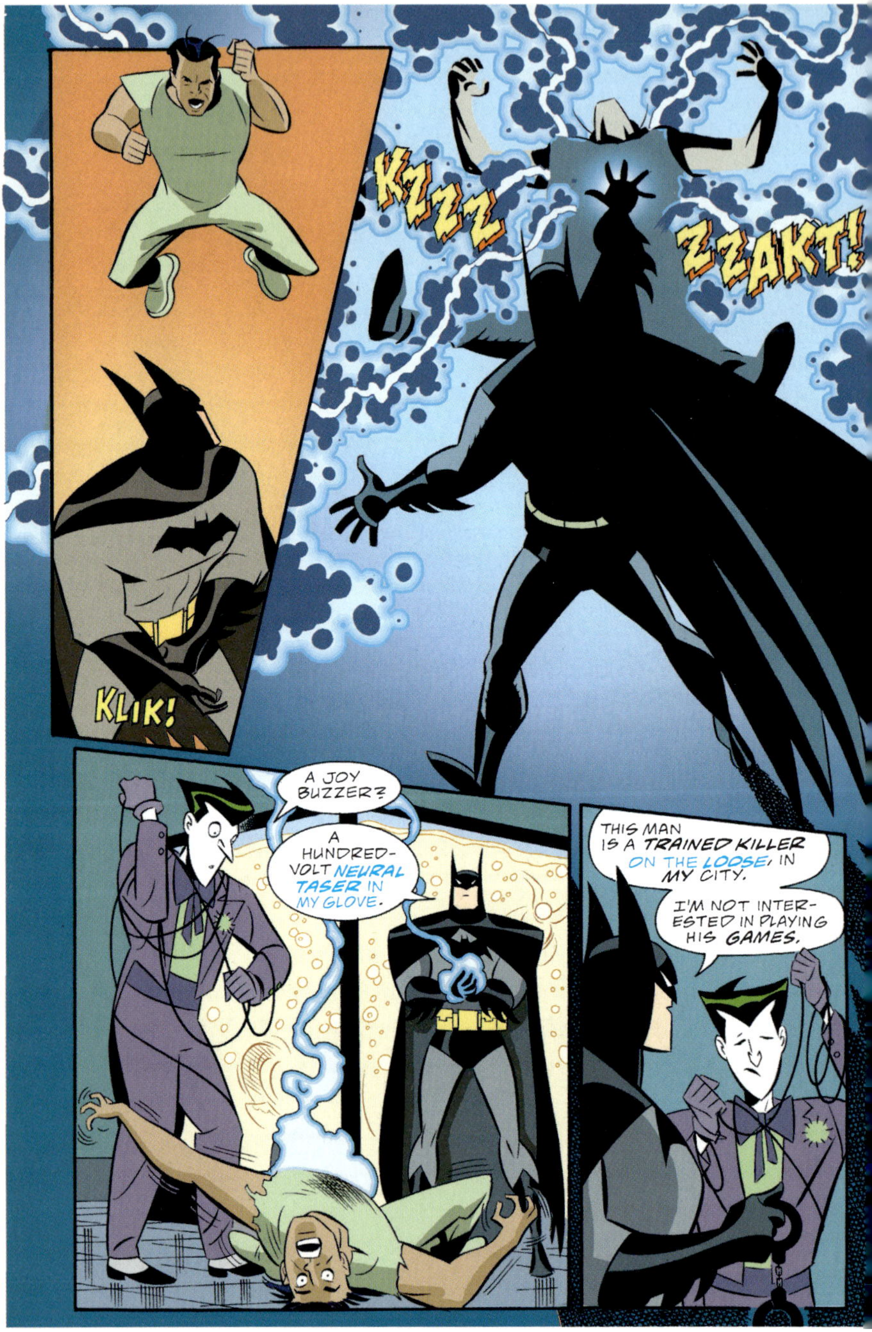

KZZZZ
ZZAKT!
KLIK!
A JOY BUZZER?
A HUNDRED-VOLT NEURAL TASER IN MY GLOVE.
THIS MAN IS A TRAINED KILLER ON THE LOOSE, IN MY CITY.
I'M NOT INTERESTED IN PLAYING HIS GAMES.

KLONG!
ZZWIP!
HARLEY BABY!
GOOD SHOT!
DO YOU KNOW HOW TO THROW A PARTY!
DON'T TOUCH ME.
I'VE HAD ENOUGH OF YOU.
C'MERE...
I GO FOR A MAN WITH BIG EARS.
SMOOCH!
WHAT...?
GET THIS STRAIGHT, YA LUMMOX--
I LIKE BATMAN BETTER THAN YOU! ALWAYS DID!

=SNIFF=
WELL...
IF THAT'S THE WAY YOU FEEL...
...THEN I'LL JUST HAVE TO RIP BATMAN'S LUNGS OUT THROUGH HIS EARS!!
Tee hee...
KICK!
CAN'T HAVE YOU ZAPPING ME WITH YOUR LITTLE TOY, CAN WE?
CRUNCH!
UNH!

POW!
IT WORKED!
IT WORKED! IT WORKED! OH, MISTAH J!
LOOK AT THAT! BAT-BOY HAS HIS HANDS AROUND MY CROSSBOW...
WHAT, ARE YOU GOING TO HEAD-BUTT ME WITH MY OWN HEAD?
I'M SO SCARED!
SLAM!
HAAAA HA HA HA...
HIT HIM AGAIN, PUDDIN'! HE'S STILL MOVING!
NOT NOW, HARLEY...
...DADDY'S BUSY!

MISSED!
THAT'S YOUR ONE FREE SHOT!
THUNK!
KRAK...
SPLOORG!
UH-OH.
SHLOOOSH!
SHLUBOOSH!

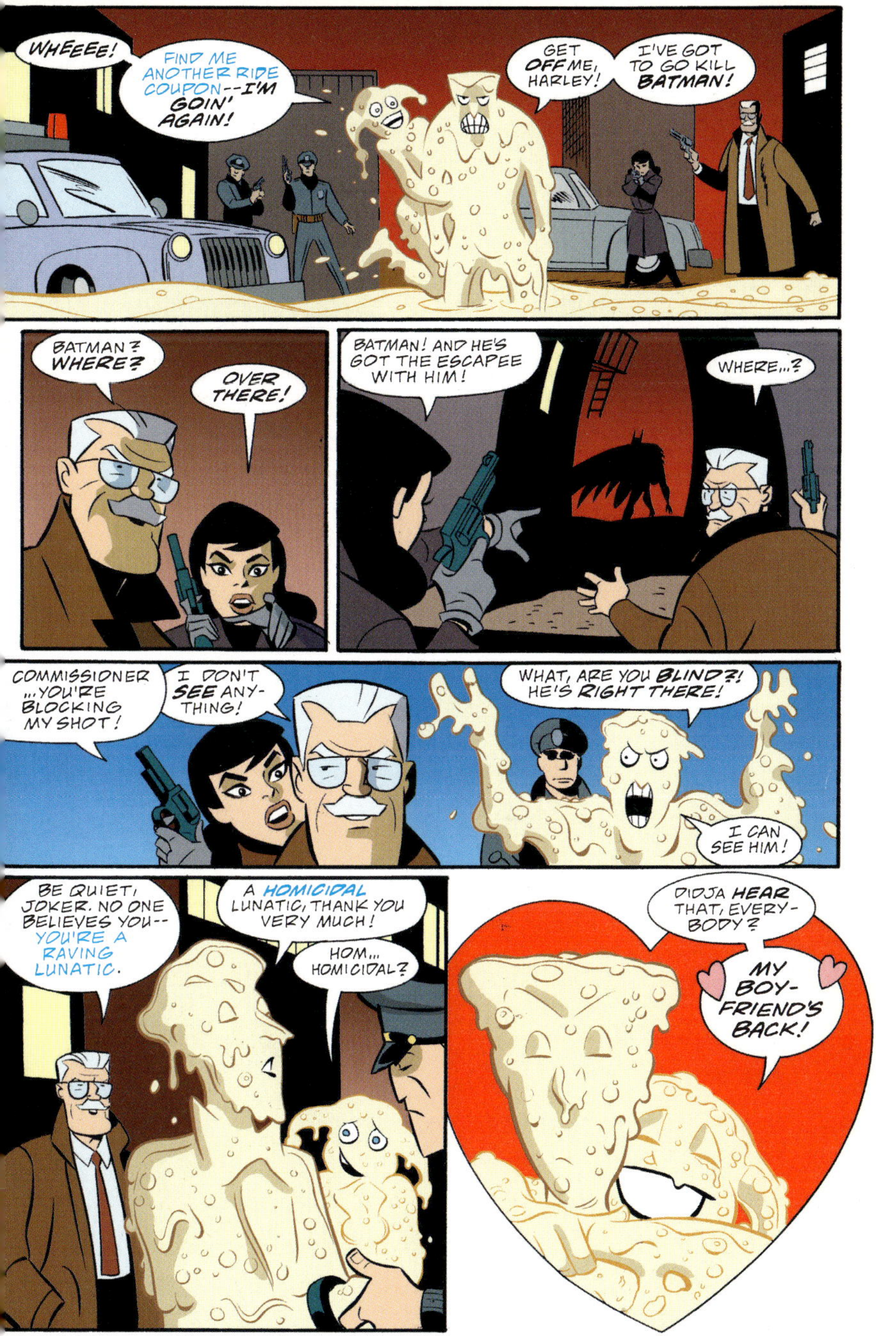
WHEEEE!
FIND ME ANOTHER RIDE COUPON--I'M GOIN' AGAIN!
GET OFF ME, HARLEY!
I'VE GOT TO GO KILL BATMAN!
BATMAN? WHERE?
OVER THERE!
BATMAN! AND HE'S GOT THE ESCAPEE WITH HIM!
WHERE...?
COMMISSIONER ...YOU'RE BLOCKING MY SHOT!
I DON'T SEE ANY-THING!
WHAT, ARE YOU BLIND?! HE'S RIGHT THERE!
I CAN SEE HIM!
BE QUIET, JOKER. NO ONE BELIEVES YOU-- YOU'RE A RAVING LUNATIC.
A HOMICIDAL LUNATIC, THANK YOU VERY MUCH!
HOM... HOMICIDAL?
DIDJA HEAR THAT, EVERY-BODY?
MY BOY-FRIEND'S BACK!

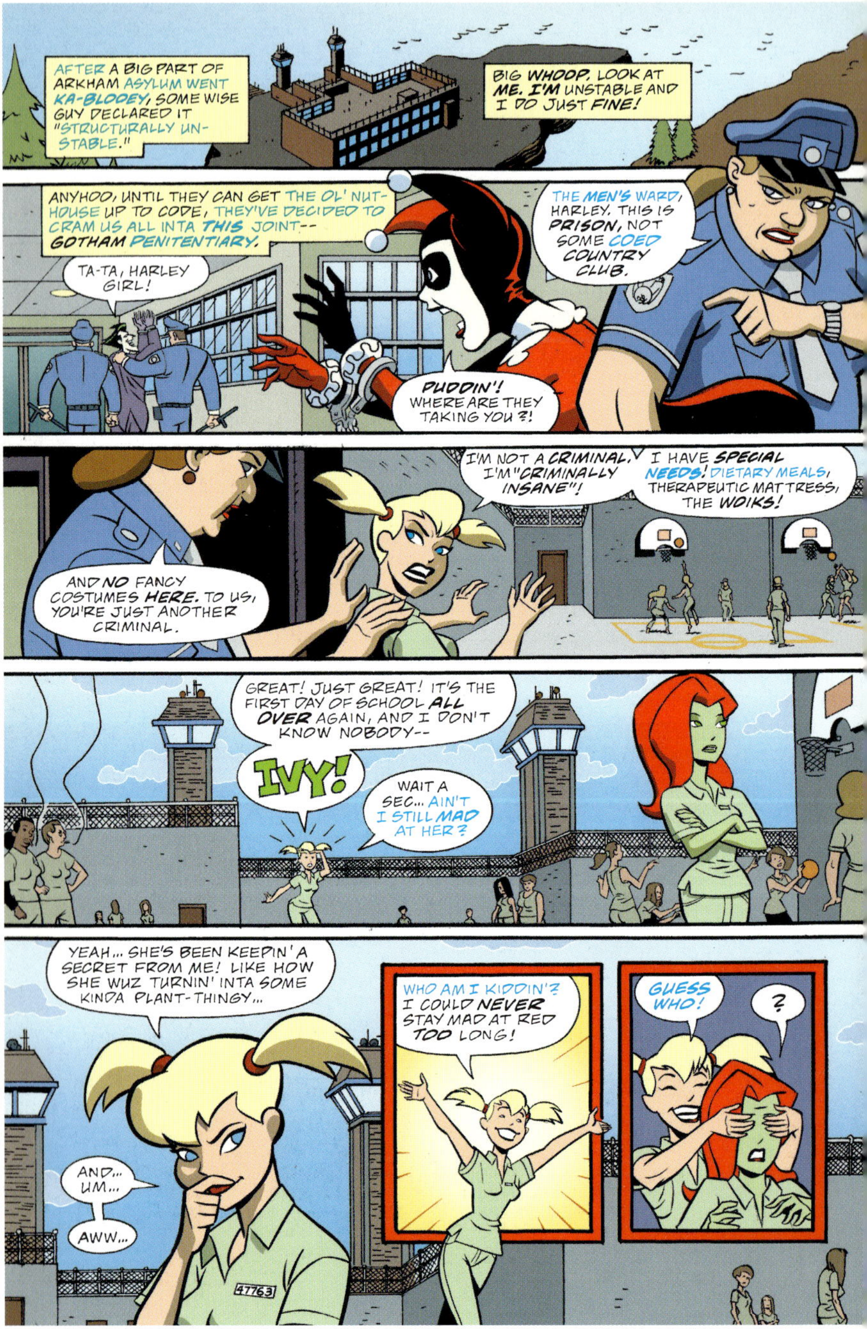
AFTER A BIG PART OF ARKHAM ASYLUM WENT KA-BLOOEY, SOME WISE GUY DECLARED IT "STRUCTURALLY UN-STABLE."
BIG WHOOP. LOOK AT ME. I'M UNSTABLE AND I DO JUST FINE!
ANYHOO, UNTIL THEY CAN GET THE OL' NUT-HOUSE UP TO CODE, THEY'VE DECIDED TO CRAM US ALL INTA THIS JOINT-- GOTHAM PENITENTIARY.
TA-TA, HARLEY GIRL!
THE MEN'S WARD, HARLEY. THIS IS PRISON, NOT SOME COED COUNTRY CLUB.
PUDDIN'! WHERE ARE THEY TAKING YOU?!
I'M NOT A CRIMINAL. I'M "CRIMINALLY INSANE"!
I HAVE SPECIAL NEEDS! DIETARY MEALS, THERAPEUTIC MATTRESS, THE WOIKS!
AND NO FANCY COSTUMES HERE. TO US, YOU'RE JUST ANOTHER CRIMINAL.
GREAT! JUST GREAT! IT'S THE FIRST DAY OF SCHOOL ALL OVER AGAIN, AND I DON'T KNOW NOBODY--
IVY!
WAIT A SEC... AIN'T I STILL MAD AT HER?
YEAH... SHE'S BEEN KEEPIN' A SECRET FROM ME! LIKE HOW SHE WUZ TURNIN' INTA SOME KINDA PLANT-THINGY...
AND... UM...
AWW...
47763
WHO AM I KIDDIN'? I COULD NEVER STAY MAD AT RED TOO LONG!
GUESS WHO!
?

GET
AWAY
FROM
ME
YOU STINKING BAG OF MEAT!
RRRRRIP
RESTRAIN HER!
THAT'S IT! IT'S SOLITARY FOR YOU, IVY!
DON'T LET THOSE THINGS TOUCH YOU!
THEY'RE POISONOUS!
P-P-POISON?
B-BUT RED WOULD NEVER POISON...
MEHHH...

HUH?
WHERE AM I? WHO'S THE PRESIDENT?
SERIOUSLY, I DIDN'T VOTE. WHO WON?
EMERGENCY! CODE RED!
WHAT'S THE HUBBUB?
ALL PRISON INFIRMARY STAFF TO POISON IVY'S CELL! SHE'S CRASHING!
IVY'S IN TROUBLE? I GOTTA--
HOO-MOMMA!
I AIN'T FELT THIS BAD SINCE MISTAH J MADE ME WEAR THE PIÑATA SUIT...
WOW, SHE MUST REALLY BE SICK! THAT EXPLAINS EVERYTHING!
THERE'S NO WAY IVY WOULD REALLY HURT ME...
ISOLATION WARD 3
SUIT UP!
HANG ON. I'M A-COMIN'...
HEH. CHECK IT OUT...
...THE NEW HARLEY AND I.V. TEAM!
ONLY BIO-CONTAINMENT SUITS PAST THIS POINT!
SKWEEK! SKWEEK!

Vokabelerklärungen (S. 92–101)

S. 92/93

pure oxygen [pjur ˈahxidschən] reiner Sauerstoff
is breathing in … [is ˈbrihðing in] atmet … ein
she detests [schi diˈteßtß] dass sie verabscheut
without us, she'll suffocate [wiðˈaut aß schil ˈsafəkäit] ohne uns wird sie ersticken
roomies [ˈruhmis] Zimmergenossinnen
handpicked by the immortal … [ˈhändpikt bai ði iˈmohrtəl] auserwählt von der Hand des unsterblichen …
targets [ˈtahrgətß] Ziele
value their deaths [ˈvälju ðer deθß] schätzt ihren Tod

S. 94/95

on your quest you may cross paths with … [ahn jur kweßt ju mäi krahß pähθß wið] auf eurer Suche kreuzen sich vielleicht eure Wege mit denen von …
I have yet to see his equal [ai həv jet tə ßih his ˈihkwəl] bin ich noch niemandem begegnet, der es mit ihm aufnehmen könnte
Truly, a worthy foe! [ˈtruhli ə ˈwöhrði fou] Wahrhaftig, ein würdiger Gegner!
Engage him if you must. [inˈgäidsch him if ju maßt] Befasst euch mit ihm, wenn es sein muss.
But he is not to be harmed. [bat hi is naht tə bi hahrmd] Aber er darf nicht verletzt werden.
I swore his will would be done. [ai ßwohr his wil wud bi dan] Ich habe geschworen, dass ich seinem Willen gehorchen würde.
on the field of battle [ahn ðə fihld əv bätl] auf dem Schlachtfeld
unconsciousness [anˈkahnschəßnəß] Bewusstlosigkeit
like a coward [laik ə ˈkauərd] wie ein Feigling

S. 96/97

You lack a killer's heart! [ju läk ə ˈkilərs hahrt] Du hast nicht das Herz eines Killers!
magnify [ˈmägnifai] vergrößern
a rare skin mite [ə rer ßkin mait] eine seltene Hautmilbe
return our "guest" to the authorities [riˈtöhrn ˈauər geßt tə ði əˈθahritis] gib unseren „Gast" an die Behörden zurück
we'll take off once we've refueled [wihl täik ahf wanß wiv riˈfjuəld] wir fliegen los, sobald wir aufgetankt haben

S. 98/99

if I recall [if ai riˈkahl] wenn ich mich recht erinnere
he's forgotten [hihs fərˈgahtn] er hat es vergessen
I am to convey his deep regrets. [ai äm tə kənˈväi his dihp riˈgretß] Ich soll sein tief empfundenes Bedauern übermitteln.

S. 100/101

advantage [ədˈväntidsch] Vorteil

▶ *Nächste Ausklappseite: S. 111*

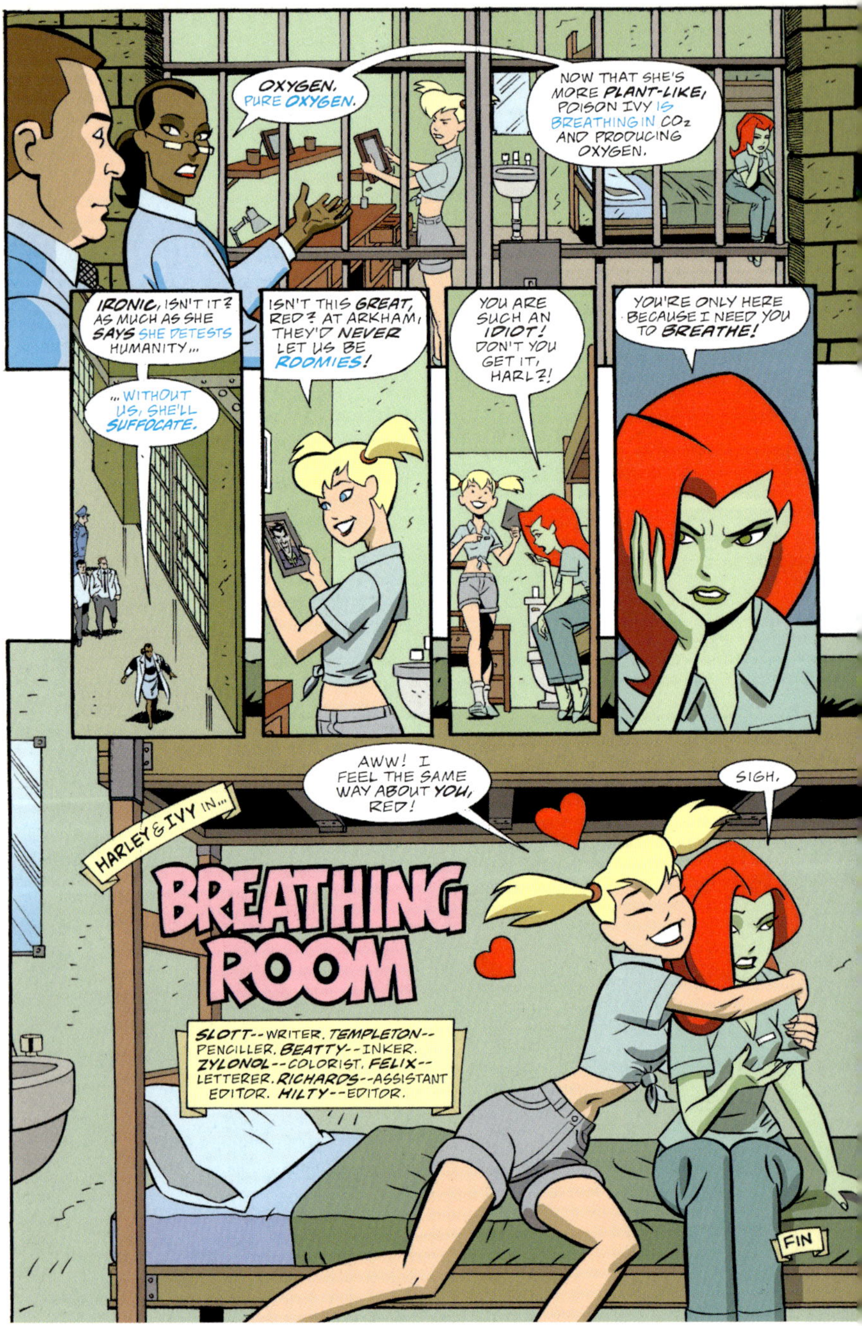
OXYGEN. PURE OXYGEN.
NOW THAT SHE'S MORE PLANT-LIKE, POISON IVY IS BREATHING IN CO2 AND PRODUCING OXYGEN.
IRONIC, ISN'T IT? AS MUCH AS SHE SAYS SHE DETESTS HUMANITY...
...WITHOUT US, SHE'LL SUFFOCATE.
ISN'T THIS GREAT, RED? AT ARKHAM, THEY'D NEVER LET US BE ROOMIES!
YOU ARE SUCH AN IDIOT! DON'T YOU GET IT, HARL?!
YOU'RE ONLY HERE BECAUSE I NEED YOU TO BREATHE!
AWW! I FEEL THE SAME WAY ABOUT YOU, RED!
SIGH.
HARLEY & IVY IN...
BREATHING ROOM
SLOTT--WRITER. TEMPLETON--PENCILLER. BEATTY--INKER. ZYLONOL--COLORIST. FELIX--LETTERER. RICHARDS--ASSISTANT EDITOR. HILTY--EDITOR.
FIN

THERE. THAT ONE LOOKS PROMISING.
I AM HASSAN. HAND-PICKED BY THE IMMORTAL RA'S AL GHUL.
AS A MEMBER OF HIS SOCIETY OF SHADOWS, MINE WAS A LIFETIME OF TRAINING, DISCIPLINE...
...AND SECRET ARTS.
IT IS TIME.
I LIVED TO SERVE--AND DESIRED NOTHING ELSE.
SLOTT-TEMPLETON-BEATTY-ZYLONOL-FELIX-RICHARDS AND HILTY PRESENT...
NEED TO KNOW
BANE
SCARECROW
VENTRILOQUIST
RIDDLER
KILLER CROC
POISON IVY
MR. FREEZE
JOKER
TWO-FACE
MAD HATTER
THESE ARE YOUR NEW TARGETS.
VALUE THEIR DEATHS MORE THAN YOU VALUE YOUR OWN LIFE.

ON YOUR QUEST, YOU MAY CROSS PATHS WITH THE DETECTIVE.
IN ALL MY YEARS, I HAVE YET TO SEE HIS EQUAL. TRULY, A WORTHY FOE!
ENGAGE HIM IF YOU MUST-- BUT HE IS NOT TO BE HARMED.
MY REASONS FOR THIS ARE MY OWN. THAT IS ALL YOU NEED TO KNOW.
NEVER HAD I HEARD THE MASTER GIVE SUCH PRAISE!
I SWORE HIS WILL WOULD BE DONE.
THOUGH IN MY HEART, I HOPED TO MEET THIS DETECTIVE ON THE FIELD OF BATTLE.
AND I DID! BUT NOT FACE TO FACE...
WHAM!
ZAK!
...OR HAND TO HAND!
SLIPPING INTO UNCONSCIOUSNESS, I KNEW I'D BEEN CHEATED! LIED TO!
FOR THIS IS NO WORTHY FOE!
WH-WHAT?!

I SAID--
--WHERE CAN I FIND RA'S AL GHUL?
NO!
TWICE I HAVE FACED YOU! AND EACH TIME YOU FOUGHT LIKE A COWARD!
I AM NOT AFRAID OF YOU!
TALK OR I'LL--
OR YOU'LL WHAT? THROW ME OFF THIS CLIFF?
DO IT!

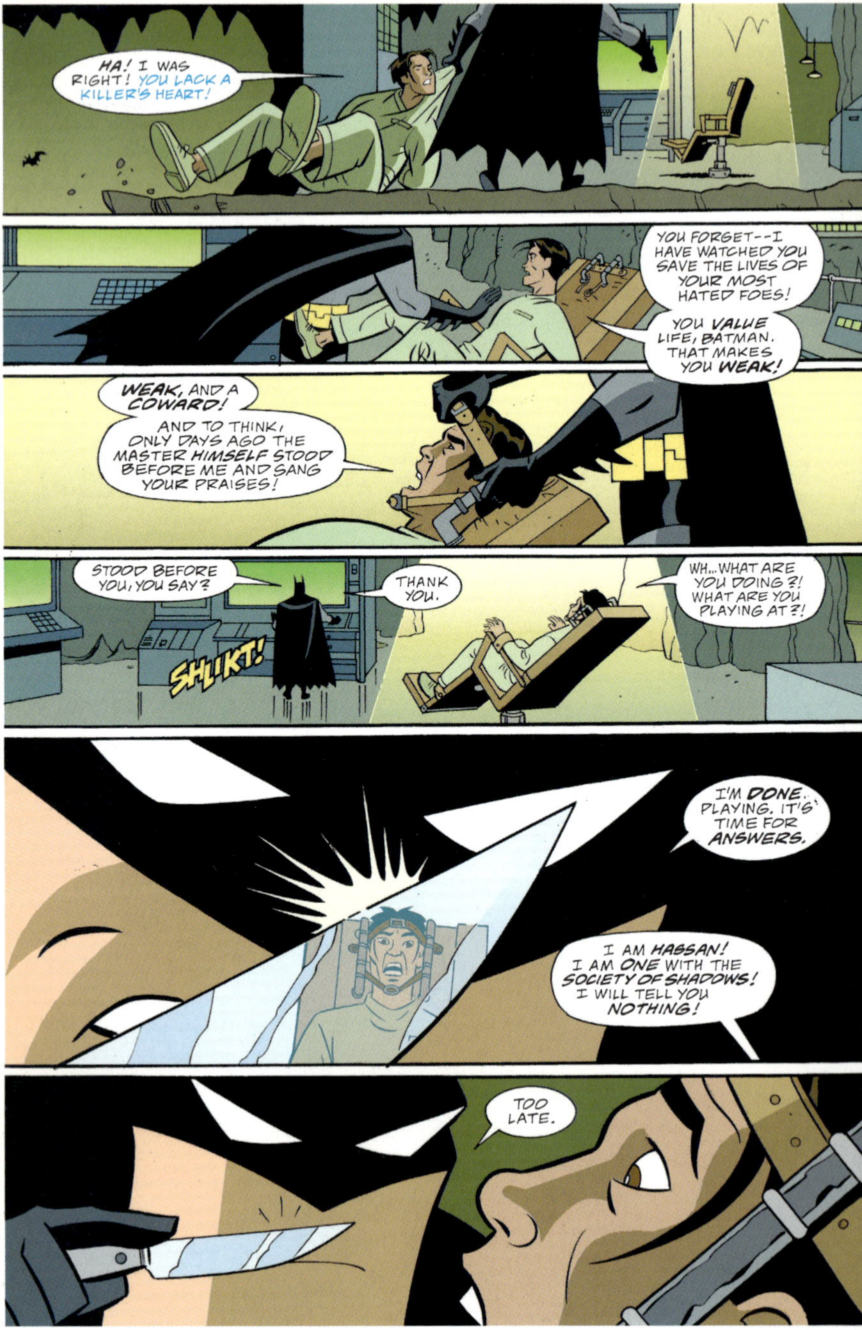
HA! I WAS RIGHT! YOU LACK A KILLER'S HEART!
YOU FORGET--I HAVE WATCHED YOU SAVE THE LIVES OF YOUR MOST HATED FOES!
YOU VALUE LIFE, BATMAN. THAT MAKES YOU WEAK!
WEAK, AND A COWARD!
AND TO THINK, ONLY DAYS AGO THE MASTER HIMSELF STOOD BEFORE ME AND SANG YOUR PRAISES!
STOOD BEFORE YOU, YOU SAY?
THANK YOU.
SHLIKT!
WH...WHAT ARE YOU DOING?! WHAT ARE YOU PLAYING AT?!
I'M DONE PLAYING. IT'S TIME FOR ANSWERS.
I AM HASSAN! I AM ONE WITH THE SOCIETY OF SHADOWS! I WILL TELL YOU NOTHING!
TOO LATE.

SCRAPE! SCRAPE!
SCRAPE!
SCRAPE! SCRAPE!
YOU'VE ALREADY TOLD ME EVERY-THING I NEED TO KNOW.
COMPUTER, SCAN FOR MICRO-ORGANISMS.
KLIK!
ANALYZING.
ANALYSIS COMPLETE.
THERE. THAT ONE'S PROMISING. MAGNIFY.
YES, A RARE SKIN MITE, EXCLUSIVE TO THE ISLAND OF MANGAREVA.
NO!
BATGIRL, RETURN OUR "GUEST" TO THE AUTHORITIES.
ROBIN, YOU'RE WITH ME. WE'LL TAKE OFF ONCE WE'VE REFUELED THE BATPLANE.
GOTCHA.
SEE YOU AROUND, HASSAN! KEEP YOUR NOSE CLEAN! AND DON'T WORRY...
"...WE'LL BE SURE TO SEND RA'S YOUR REGARDS!"
THE END

THE BALANCE

TY TEMPLETON — WRITER
RICK BURCHETT — PENCILLER
TERRY BEATTY — INKER
LEE LOUGHRIDGE — COLORIST
PHIL FELIX — LETTERER
HARVEY RICHARDS — ASSISTANT
JOAN HILTY — EDITOR
BATMAN CREATED BY BOB KANE

EASTER ISLAND, IN THE SOUTH PACIFIC...
SUNDOWN.
SONOGRAM CONFIRMS IT.
THIS MOAI STATUE IS HOLLOW.
AND DIRECTLY OVER AN UNDER-GROUND CHAMBER.
I'VE GOT A SEAM RUNNING BELOW THE ROCK FACE... IT GOES...
KLIK!
THERE. I'VE TRIPPED A SECRET OPENING... I'M GOING IN.
YOU PROBABLY TRIPPED A DOZEN ALARMS AS WELL.
I COULD BE MORE HELP TO YOU ON THE GROUND, INSTEAD OF FLYING THE BAT-TAXI...
NO.
RA'S AL GHUL IS THE MOST RUTH-LESS MAN ALIVE, ROBIN.
YOU DON'T FACE HIM.
YOU HOVER AND WAIT FOR INSTRUCTIONS.

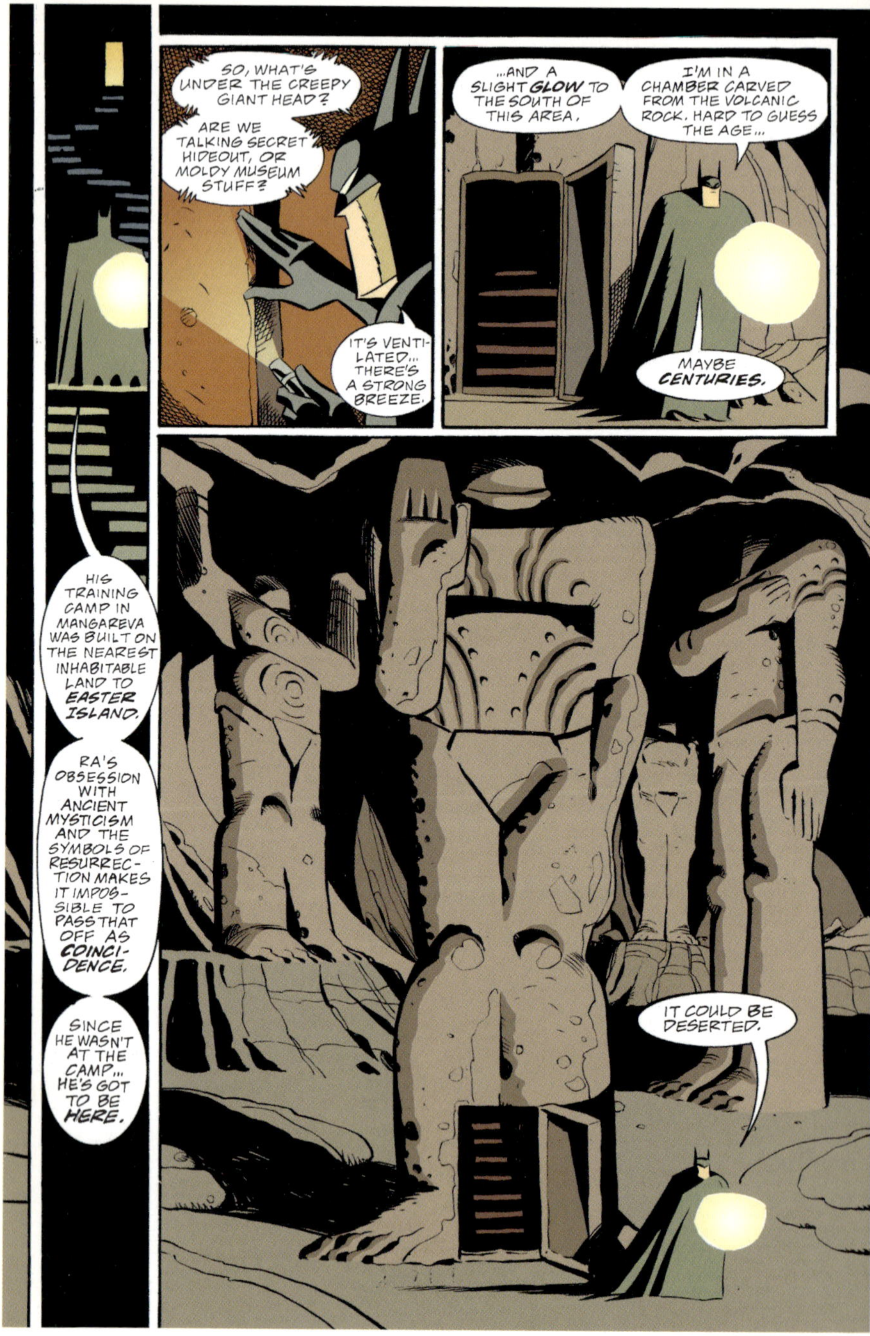
SO, WHAT'S UNDER THE CREEPY GIANT HEAD?
ARE WE TALKING SECRET HIDEOUT, OR MOLDY MUSEUM STUFF?
IT'S VENTILATED... THERE'S A STRONG BREEZE.
...AND A SLIGHT GLOW TO THE SOUTH OF THIS AREA.
I'M IN A CHAMBER CARVED FROM THE VOLCANIC ROCK. HARD TO GUESS THE AGE...
MAYBE CENTURIES.
HIS TRAINING CAMP IN MANGAREVA WAS BUILT ON THE NEAREST INHABITABLE LAND TO EASTER ISLAND.
RA'S OBSESSION WITH ANCIENT MYSTICISM AND THE SYMBOLS OF RESURRECTION MAKES IT IMPOSSIBLE TO PASS THAT OFF AS COINCIDENCE.
SINCE HE WASN'T AT THE CAMP... HE'S GOT TO BE HERE.
IT COULD BE DESERTED.

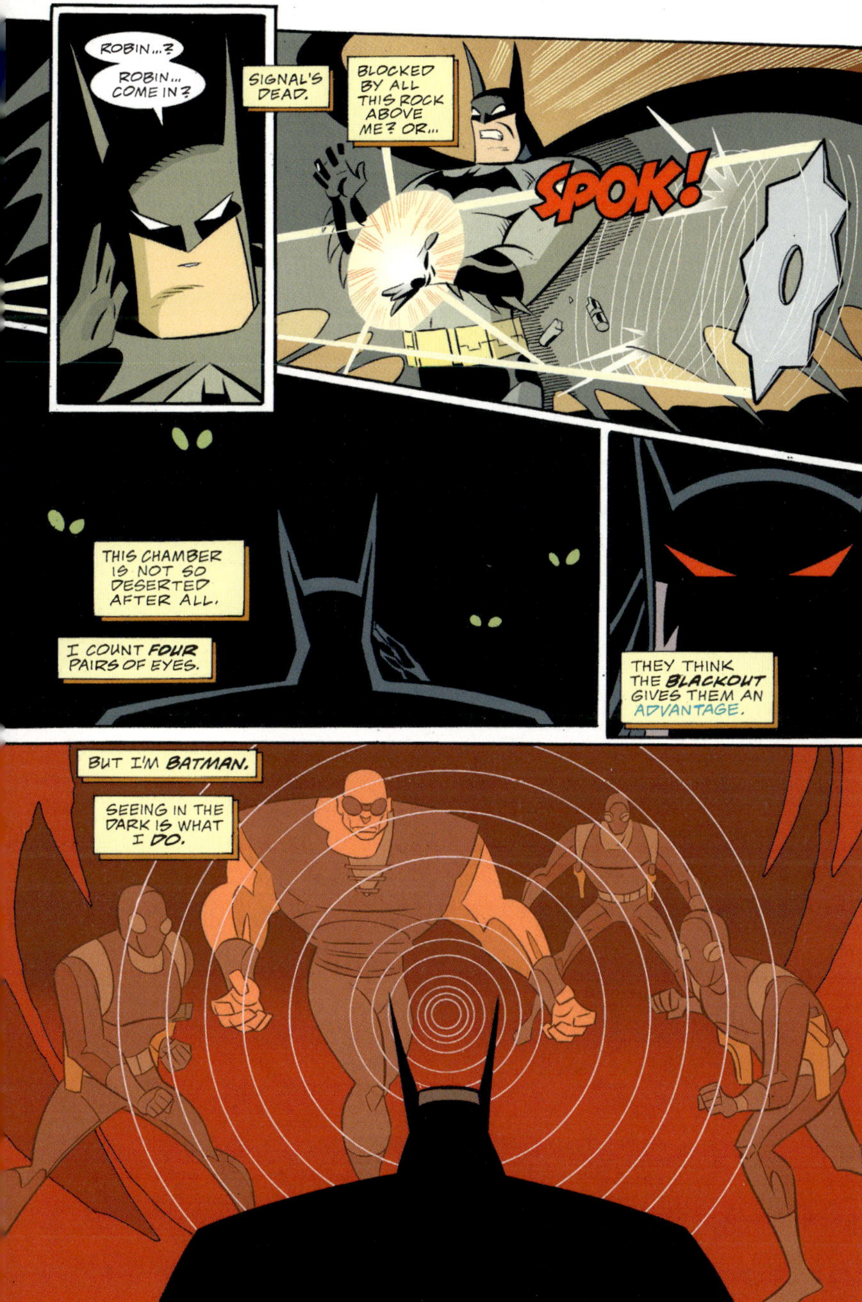
ROBIN...?
ROBIN... COME IN?
SIGNAL'S DEAD.
BLOCKED BY ALL THIS ROCK ABOVE ME? OR...
SPOK!
THIS CHAMBER IS NOT SO DESERTED AFTER ALL.
I COUNT FOUR PAIRS OF EYES.
THEY THINK THE BLACKOUT GIVES THEM AN ADVANTAGE.
BUT I'M BATMAN.
SEEING IN THE DARK IS WHAT I DO.

SOMEONE ELSE IN THE ROOM.
PERFUME ON THE BREEZE...
...ROSES?
GGKK!
HWK!
TALIA.
≡SIGH!≡ YOU AND MY FATHER.
WHAT AM I GOING TO DO WITH YOU?

THE UNMISTAKABLE SMELL OF ROTTING MEAT AND JASMINE WAKES ME.
I'M NEAR A LAZARUS PIT.
ONE OF THE MYSTERIOUS HEALING POOLS IN WHICH RA'S AL GHUL IMMERSES HIMSELF IN ORDER TO REMAIN IMMORTAL.
THESE PITS HAVE KEPT HIM ALIVE FOR CENTURIES--BUT THEY LONG AGO DROVE HIM MAD.
RAPA NUI IS SACRED TO ME, DETECTIVE.
I'VE RETURNED HERE OFTEN SINCE MY YEARS WITH CAPTAIN COOK AND THE BRITISH NAVY...
THIS TRAGIC ISLAND IS NEVER FAR FROM MY THOUGHTS.
BUT WHY ARE YOU HERE? WHY NOW?
BECAUSE YOU WEREN'T AT YOUR BASE ON MANGA-REVA.
I'M AMAZED YOU DIS-COVERED THAT INSTALLATION. NO DOUBT THAT'S WHY WE LOST CONTACT WITH THEM...
YOU SENT SHADOW ASSASSINS FROM THERE TO GOTHAM. TRIED TO KILL JOKER, TWO-FACE, POISON IVY, RIDDLER...
WHY?
ARE YOU MOVING INTO GOTHAM AND ELIMINATING THE COMPETITION?
NO.
SETTLING A VENDETTA?
NO.

NO VENDETTAS.
IT WAS A GIFT.
FOR YOU.
MURDER...
...IS A GIFT?
OF PEOPLE SUCH AS YOU MENTIONED...? ABSOLUTELY.
I'M CENTURIES OLD, DETECTIVE, AND I SUPPOSE SOMEWHAT SENTIMENTAL.
AS MUCH TIME AS I DEVOTE TO RESCUING THIS POOR, BELEAGUERED PLANET FROM THE DEATH GRIP HUMANITY HAS UPON IT...
...I SPEND AN EQUAL AMOUNT OF TIME CONSIDERING MY DAUGHTER.
YOU'RE VERY IMPORTANT TO HER. SHE SEES GREAT-NESS IN YOU.
SOMETIMES I WONDER IF IT'S NOT ALL JUST TO IRRITATE HER FATHER...
BUT WHERE SHE SEES GREAT-NESS, I SEE A GREAT MANY DIS-TRACTIONS.
SO I CHOSE TO REMOVE THEM FOR YOU, AS A GESTURE OF GOODWILL BETWEEN US. SIMPLY THAT.

CALL IT OFF!
NO ONE DIES FOR ME!
COME NOW, BRUCE. YOU'VE NEVER WISHED THEM DEAD...EVEN FOR JUST A MOMENT?
MY FATHER OFFERS TO SOLVE ALL YOUR PROBLEMS...
...AND YOU GET TO KEEP THE BLOOD AWAY FROM YOUR HANDS.
YOU AND I CAN FINALLY FIND THE TIME TO --
TALIA...
YOU'RE AS SICK AS HE IS.
BELOVED...?
YOU'RE ABLE TO STAND? THE POTION IN THAT DART--
...WAS AN OLD FORMULA I'D FOUND AN ANTI-TOXIN FOR MONTHS AGO.
RA'S--
--I'VE HAD IT WITH YOU PLAYING GOD!
WHAT...?

POW!
YOU STRUCK ME?
TO WHAT END? YOU'RE OUTNUMBERED, OUTGUNNED...
BECAUSE YOU'RE COMING BACK WITH ME THIS TIME.
YOU'RE GOING TO PAY FOR YOUR CRIMES, ONCE AND FOR ALL!
PREPOSTEROUS.
UBU-- KILL HIM SWIFTLY.
COME, DAUGHTER-- YOU SHOULDN'T SEE THIS.

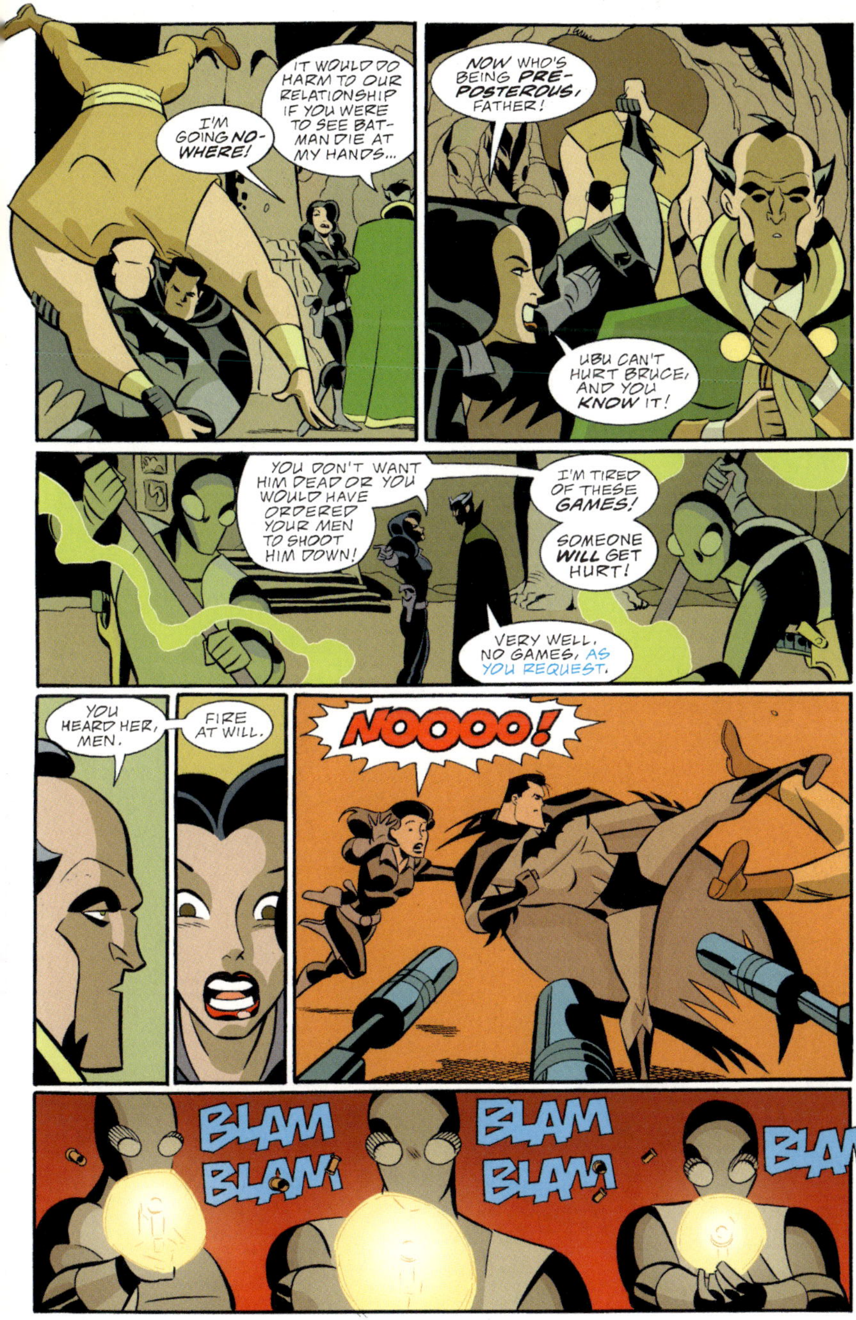
I'M GOING NO-WHERE!
IT WOULD DO HARM TO OUR RELATIONSHIP IF YOU WERE TO SEE BAT-MAN DIE AT MY HANDS...
NOW WHO'S BEING PRE-POSTEROUS, FATHER!
UBU CAN'T HURT BRUCE, AND YOU KNOW IT!
YOU DON'T WANT HIM DEAD OR YOU WOULD HAVE ORDERED YOUR MEN TO SHOOT HIM DOWN!
I'M TIRED OF THESE GAMES!
SOMEONE WILL GET HURT!
VERY WELL. NO GAMES, AS YOU REQUEST.
YOU HEARD HER, MEN.
FIRE AT WILL.
NOOOO!
BLAM
BLAM
BLAM
BLAM
BLAM

NO!
THUK!
THUK!
THUK!
BE...
BELOVED...?
I...
TALIA!
NO...
UHHH...

WE SHOT THE DAUGHTER.
WE WERE ORDERED TO FIRE.
WILL IT MATTER?
RA'S WILL KILL US ALL!
STOP! IT IS YOUR DUTY TO DIE FOR THE MASTER, COWARDS!
YOU STAY AND DO YOUR DUTY, THEN!
THERE'S STILL A CHANCE!
SHE'S FALLEN INTO THE LAZARUS PIT--ITS HEALING POWERS SHOULD SAVE HER!
IF SHE IS STRONG ENOUGH TO SURVIVE THE BLOOD MADNESS THAT FOLLOWS...
DAUGHTER...?
GRAAAAAH!

UBU. SHE MUST BE SUBDUED WITH GREAT CARE.
SHE IS NOT IN CONTROL OF HER MIND AT THE MOMENT...
GRAAAGHH!
WHAM!
GAAAHH!
TALIA.
I AM YOUR FATHER.
IF YOU FOCUS.
RRRR...
LISTEN TO THE SOUND OF MY VOICE AND YOU CAN CONQUER THIS FEVER...

Vokabelerklärungen (S. 112–114)

S. 112/113

my legs give out [mai legs giv aut] meine Beine versagen
I hope … is in worse shape [ai houp … is in wöhrß schäip] ich hoffe … ist in noch schlechterer Verfassung
barely [ˈberli] kaum
raise my hand [räis mai händ] meine Hand erheben
defenseless [diˈfenßleß] wehrlos
her shameful moment [hör ˈschäimful ˈmoumənt] ihren beschämenden Moment
She won't forgive it. [schi wount fərˈgiv it] Sie wird das nicht verzeihen.
you're not escaping justice anymore [jur naht iˈßkäiping ˈdschaßtiß eniˈmohr] du entkommst der Gerechtigkeit nicht mehr
that hurts [ðät höhrtß] das tut weh
and she means that little [ənd schi mihns ðät lidl] und sie bedeutet dir so wenig

S. 114

I awoke [ai əˈwouk] ich wachte auf
to investigate [tə inˈveßtigäit] um Nachforschungen anzustellen
Is there a message for me? [is ðer ə ˈmeßidsch fər mih] Gibt es eine Nachricht für mich?

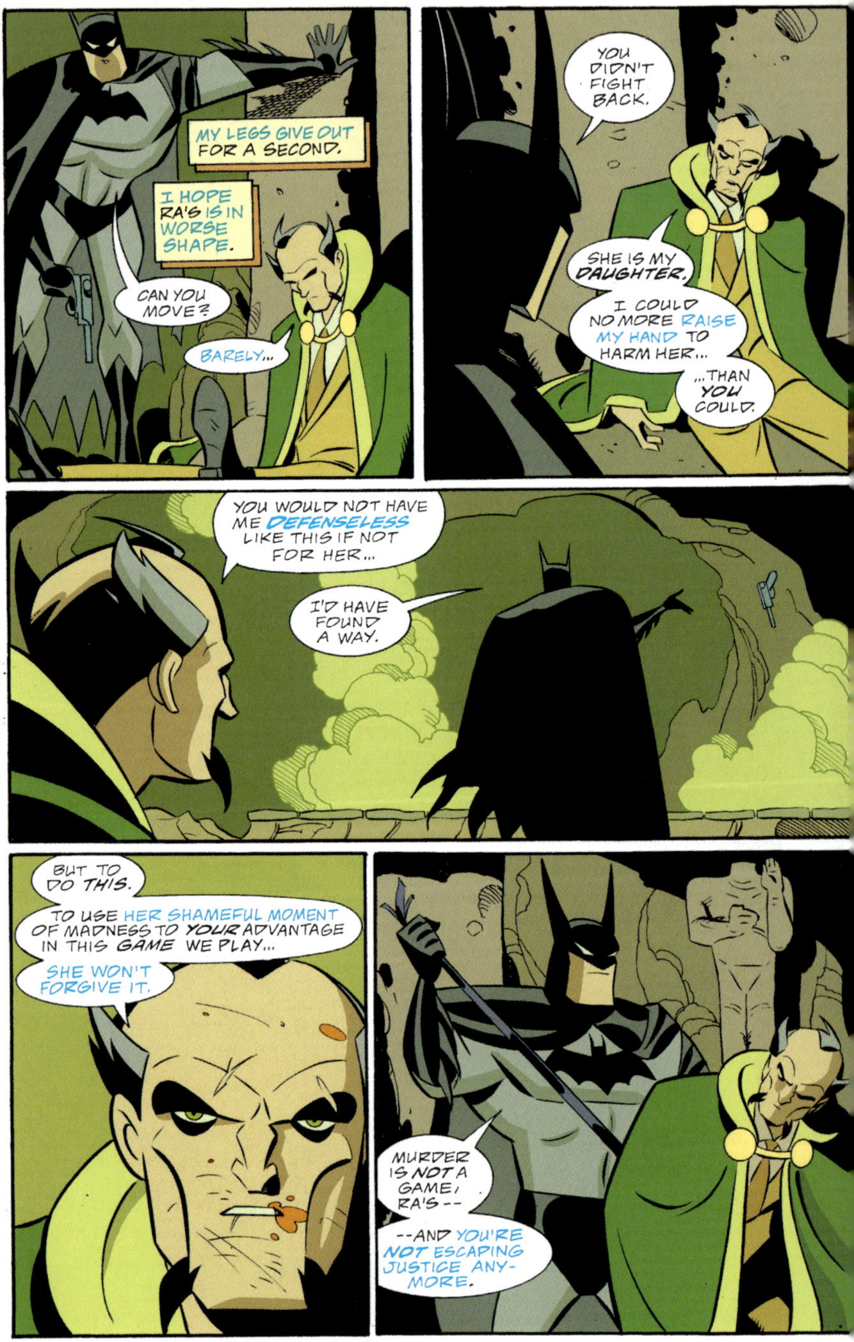
MY LEGS GIVE OUT FOR A SECOND.
I HOPE RA'S IS IN WORSE SHAPE.
CAN YOU MOVE?
BARELY...
YOU DIDN'T FIGHT BACK.
SHE IS MY DAUGHTER.
I COULD NO MORE RAISE MY HAND TO HARM HER...
...THAN YOU COULD.
YOU WOULD NOT HAVE ME DEFENSELESS LIKE THIS IF NOT FOR HER...
I'D HAVE FOUND A WAY.
BUT TO DO THIS.
TO USE HER SHAMEFUL MOMENT OF MADNESS TO YOUR ADVANTAGE IN THIS GAME WE PLAY...
SHE WON'T FORGIVE IT.
MURDER IS NOT A GAME, RA'S --
--AND YOU'RE NOT ESCAPING JUSTICE ANY-MORE.

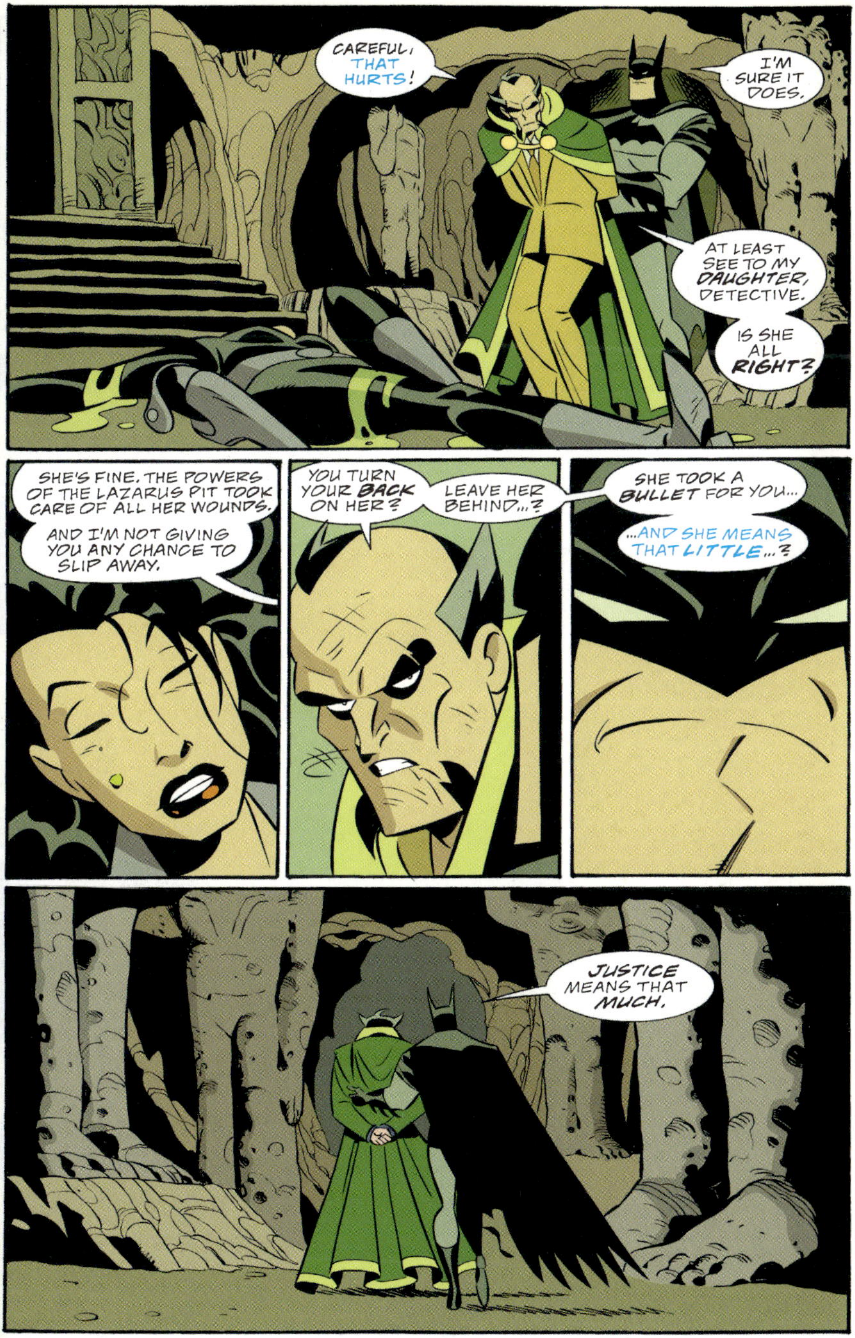
CAREFUL, THAT HURTS!
I'M SURE IT DOES.
AT LEAST SEE TO MY DAUGHTER, DETECTIVE.
IS SHE ALL RIGHT?
SHE'S FINE. THE POWERS OF THE LAZARUS PIT TOOK CARE OF ALL HER WOUNDS.
AND I'M NOT GIVING YOU ANY CHANCE TO SLIP AWAY.
YOU TURN YOUR BACK ON HER?
LEAVE HER BEHIND...?
SHE TOOK A BULLET FOR YOU...
...AND SHE MEANS THAT LITTLE...?
JUSTICE MEANS THAT MUCH.

MMM...
UBU?
WHERE IS MY FATHER?
I DO NOT KNOW. I AWOKE ONLY MOMENTS BEFORE YOU.
THE DETECTIVE IS GONE ALSO.
WE SHOULD BE MOVING FROM HERE...
THE THICK SMOKE FROM THIS MOAI WILL BRING PEOPLE TO INVESTIGATE.
IS THERE A MESSAGE FOR ME? FROM--
NO MESSAGE.
NO MESSAGE...?
WHY WOULD HE DO THAT TO ME?
The End

Inhaltsangaben

Wiederholungstäter (S. 5–26)

Batman hat Catwoman bei einem Einbruch in eine Villa auf frischer Tat ertappt. Als sie ihm versichert, dass sie nicht so kriminell ist, wie es scheint, glaubt er ihr nicht. Es gelingt ihr, Batman außer Gefecht zu setzen und den Tresor zu öffnen. Erschrocken stellt sie fest, dass sich dort eine Bombe befindet und sie in eine Falle geraten ist. Sie kann Batman, der ihr gefolgt ist, gerade noch wegstoßen, als der Sprengsatz explodiert. Catwoman wird dabei schwer verletzt.

Batmans Nachforschungen ergeben, dass in letzter Zeit eine Reihe von Einbrüchen verübt, aber nicht bei der Polizei angezeigt wurden. Mit Batgirls Hilfe findet er heraus, dass alle Bestohlenen reiche Männer sind, die nicht immer auf der Seite des Gesetzes stehen. Jeder von ihnen hielt sich gerade im Club *Iceberg Lounge* auf, als der Diebstahl verübt wurde. Batman und Batgirl statten dem Besitzer, Oswald Cobblepot alias Penguin, einen Besuch ab. In seinem Auftrag nämlich hat Catwoman die reichen Gäste bestohlen. Als Cobblepot aber bemerkte, dass sie einen Teil der Beute behielt, stellte er ihr eine Falle. Batman erfährt, dass Catwoman nur „rückfällig" geworden ist und Reiche bestohlen hat, um Bedürftigen zu helfen. Nach einigem Zögern entschuldigt er sich bei ihr für sein Verhalten.

Kein Asyl (S. 27–43)

Der neue Bürgermeister von Gotham City, Oswald Cobblepot, hat unmissverständlich klargemacht, dass er keinerlei Selbstjustiz in der Stadt dulden wird. Dadurch wird auch Batman zum Geächteten, der von der Polizei wie ein Verbrecher verfolgt wird.

Eine Truppe von Auftragskillern in schwarzen Kostümen überfällt die psychiatrische Anstalt, in der Poison Ivy, Two-Face, der Joker und andere ehemalige Widersacher Batmans einsitzen. Batman kann gerade noch verhindern, dass einige der Insassen von den maskierten Männern liquidiert werden. Wegen des Polizeiaufgebots ergreifen die Mitglieder des Killerkommandos die Flucht, und Batman kann keinen von ihnen fassen.

Wer bin ich? (S. 44–48)

Warum kämpft Batman so engagiert gegen Verbrechen jeglicher Art? Der Grund liegt in seiner Kindheit:

Der junge Bruce Wayne schaut sich mit seinen Eltern im Kino *Das Zeichen des Zorro* an. Der Kämpfer für Gerechtigkeit ist sein großes Vorbild. Nach dem Kinobesuch werden Bruces Eltern von einem Räuber überfallen und erschossen. Er schwört Rache und unterzieht sich einer jahrelangen Ausbildung, während der er Körper und Geist trainiert, um schließlich als Batman – wie sein Vorbild Zorro – gegen das Verbrechen zu kämpfen.

Freier Mann (S. 49–65)

Ein ehemaliger Verbrecher, Edward Nygma alias Riddler, bietet Omnicorp Communications ein Gerät an, das er für die Übermittlung von Nachrichten entwickelt hat. Das Geschäft steht vor dem Abschluss, als ein Killerkommando aus der Luft das Büro stürmt und Jagd auf den Riddler macht.

Zur selben Zeit hält sich Bruce Wayne mit Julie Madison in der Basketball-Arena auf. Auf den Übertragungsmonitoren erscheint plötzlich der Riddler, der verzweifelte Hilferufe aussendet und in einem Rätsel seinen Aufenthaltsort nennt. Bruce alias Batman macht sich sofort auf den Weg. Auch einer der schwarz gekleideten Killer hat das Rätsel gelöst und den Riddler aufgespürt. Batman kann ihn jedoch unschädlich machen. Er weiß, dass die Killer den Befehlen von Ra's al Ghul gehorchen, aber weder er noch der Riddler kennen den Grund, warum dieser Sektenführer die Mitglieder der Gothamer Unterwelt auslöschen will.

Falsches Spiel (S. 66–70)

Rupert Thorne, ein Bauunternehmer, versucht, Bürgermeister Cobblepot mit Geld zu bestechen, um an einen großen Auftrag zu kommen. Batman lässt das Gespräch aufzeichnen, weil er Cobblepot eine ungesetzmäßige Handlung nachweisen will. Dieser übermittelt den Inhalt des Gesprächs allerdings an die Polizei, und so muss Batman auf eine neue Gelegenheit warten. Der Titel der Geschichte „Fowl Play" ist ein Wortspiel. Er klingt wie „Foul Play" (= Falsches Spiel), bedeutet aber eigentlich „Geflügelspiel" (fowl = Geflügel) – eine Anspielung auf Cobblepot, der auch „penguin" genannt wird.

Mein Freund ist zurück (S. 71–87)

Harley Quinn hat ihrem Freund Joker zur Flucht aus der psychiatrischen Anstalt verholfen, muss aber feststellen, dass er nach einer Reihe von Therapieversuchen nicht mehr so ist wie früher. Um ihn dazu zu bringen, wieder ein richtiger Bösewicht zu werden, unternimmt sie alle möglichen Anstrengungen. Sie befreit sogar einen der Killer aus dem Gefängnis und setzt ihn auf den Joker an, damit dieser sich wehren muss und so seine alte Form wiederfindet. Batman, der dem Joker zu Hilfe kommt, setzt zuerst den Killer außer Gefecht und anschließend den Joker und seine Freundin Harley Quinn. Allerdings hat Harley letztendlich ihr Ziel erreicht, indem sie den Joker mit einem Liebesgeständnis an Batman eifersüchtig gemacht und dazu gebracht hat, Batman anzugreifen.

Raum zum Atmen (S. 88–92)

Nach dem Anschlag auf die psychiatrische Anstalt (Arkham Asylum) wurden die Insassen ins Gefängnis verlegt. Harley ist Poison Ivy eigentlich immer noch böse, weil diese ihr nichts von ihrer Unverwundbarkeit erzählt hat. Spontan beschließt sie aber, ihren Ärger darüber zu vergessen. Als sie Poison Ivy in kindlicher Freude von hinten die Augen zuhält, wird sie von ihr wütend angegriffen. An Poison Ivys Körper haben sich giftige Stacheln gebildet. Die Wärter überwältigen sie und bringen sie in einen abgeschlossenen Raum.

Harley wird inzwischen auf der Krankenstation versorgt. Als sie hört, dass es Poison Ivy sehr schlecht geht, macht sie sich sofort auf den Weg und stürzt an den Wachposten vorbei in die Quarantäneabteilung. Nachdem sie den Raum betreten hat, geht es Poison Ivy sofort besser. Sie hat sich bereits so weit zur Pflanze entwickelt, dass sie Kohlendioxid zum Überleben benötigt und ihrerseits reinen Sauerstoff produziert. Deshalb beschließt man, dass sich die beiden eine Zelle teilen sollen, ein Umstand, der Harley bedeutend mehr Freude bereitet als Poison Ivy.

Was man wissen muss (S. 93–97)

Die von Ra's al Ghul ausgebildeten Kämpfer gehorchen ihrem Meister bedingungslos und sind bereit, für einen Auftrag ihr Leben zu lassen. Als der von Batman überwältigte Killer nichts über seinen Herrn preisgeben will, analysiert Batman seine Hautschuppen und kann so den Aufenthaltsort von Ra's ermitteln.

Die Abrechnung (S. 98–114)

Zusammen mit Robin fliegt Batman zur Osterinsel. Dort findet er den Zugang zu einem unterirdischen Versteck und trifft auf den Sektenführer Ra's. Dieser wollte die Widersacher Batmans liquidieren, um seiner Tochter Talia einen Gefallen zu tun. Sie ist in Batman verliebt und möchte, dass er mehr Zeit mit ihr verbringt, anstatt Verbrecher zu jagen.

Als Batman droht, diesen Plan zu durchkreuzen und Ra's gefangen zu nehmen, schießen dessen Leibwächter auf ihn. Die Kugeln, die für Batman bestimmt sind, treffen aber Talia, die sich schützend vor Batman stellt. Durch die Wucht der Geschosse wird sie in die Lazarusgrube geschleudert, die eine Flüssigkeit mit großer Heilkraft enthält. Ra's ist es durch regelmäßige Bäder darin gelungen, mehrere hundert Jahre alt zu werden. Seine Tochter überlebt zwar die Schussverletzungen, muss aber nun auch die Nebenwirkungen des heilenden Bades überstehen. Von Wahnsinnsattacken getrieben greift sie ihren Vater an und wird von Batman mit ihrer eigenen Betäubungswaffe außer Gefecht gesetzt.

Batman gelingt es nun doch, den geschwächten Ra's zu verhaften, um ihn seiner gerechten Strafe zuzuführen. Ra's Tochter lässt er auf der Insel zurück.

Rätsel und Übungen

Second Timers (S. 5–26)

1 Welche der angegebenen Wörter beziehungsweise Ausdrücke haben etwas mit Diebstahl zu tun? „Packen" Sie sie in Catwomans Beutel:

coincidence
burglaries
thief
bragging
loot
breaking and entering

2 Hier können Sie beweisen, dass Ihnen kein Detail der Geschichte entgangen ist. Vervollständigen Sie die folgenden Sätze. Nur eine der angegebenen Möglichkeiten ist korrekt. Wenn Sie die entsprechenden Buchstaben richtig zusammensetzen, erhalten Sie den umgangssprachlichen Begriff für „Polizei".

1. Catwoman's personal assistant is very angry with Batman and tells him to go back to …
   G … the Iceberg Lounge.
   O … his cave.
   S … Mr. Borodin's house.
2. Mr. Borodin did not report the stolen Picassos because …
   C … he knew the thief.
   F … he had ordered the break-in himself.
   S … he did not want to admit that his security system was worthless.
3. The Iceberg Lounge is owned by …
   B … Mr. Borodin.
   C … Oswald Cobblepot.
   M … Commissioner Gordon.
4. Cobblepot set a trap for Catwoman because …
   P … she had kept some of the stolen things.
   L … he feared that she might inform the police.
   Y … she was going to tell Batman the truth about the burglaries.

Der umgangssprachliche Ausdruck für „Polizei" lautet

_ _ _ _ .

No Asylum *und* Who Am I? (S. 27–48)

3 Oft werden Wörter in bestimmten Kombinationen verwendet. Erinnern Sie sich, welche beiden Begriffe jeweils zusammengehören? Verbinden Sie die Wörterpaare:

federal	luck
keeping	engines
bad	facility
fire	promise
campaign	secrets

(federal — facility)

4 Wie viele Wörter haben Sie sich aus den beiden Episoden gemerkt? Mit der Hilfe von BRUCE WAYNE alias Batman ist es sicher nicht schwierig, die folgenden Wörter ins Englische zu übersetzen. Falls Ihnen ein Wort nicht mehr einfällt, werfen Sie einfach einen Blick auf die entsprechende Ausklappseite.

1 Körper	6 Wand
2 Versprechen	7 vielversprechend
3 Beleidigung	8 Bürgermeister
4 Suchscheinwerfer	9 Insassen
5 Feind	10 ehrlich

```
          1      B _ _ _
        2      _ R _ _ _ _ _
     3   _ _ _ U _ _
   4   _ _ _ _ C _ _ _ _ _ _
       5   _ _ E _ _

          6      W _ _ _
7   _ _ _ _ _ _ A _ _ _ _
        8    _ _ Y _ _
          9    _ N _ _ _ _ _
     10   _ _ _ E _ _
```

5 In diesem Buchstabendickicht haben sich neun englische Wörter aus den beiden genannten Batman-Episoden versteckt. Die Suchbegriffe sind waagerecht (von links nach rechts), senkrecht (von oben nach unten) oder diagonal (von links oben nach rechts unten) angeordnet.

Die entsprechenden deutschen Begriffe finden Sie hier:

Standort Auftrag Wahrzeichen Einwände Adler

Anstrengungen (sich) verstecken Gerät Anwälte

s	b	q	e	p	l	a	w	y	e	r	s
o	d	f	z	f	a	g	o	u	m	b	a
b	i	a	x	l	f	c	e	a	g	l	e
j	c	s	k	s	r	o	e	t	a	j	w
e	x	s	c	y	i	o	r	i	u	m	p
c	t	i	g	r	d	t	i	t	c	v	s
t	a	g	t	f	e	p	e	z	s	w	h
i	n	n	p	s	l	y	z	g	x	s	i
o	i	m	n	k	g	c	e	o	t	q	d
n	r	e	n	g	a	d	g	e	t	p	e
s	v	n	y	j	w	o	k	d	g	e	r
m	p	t	x	l	a	n	d	m	a	r	k

6 Ordnen Sie die unten aufgeführten Wörter nach ihrer Aussprache. Achtung: Zwei Begriffe passen jeweils zu keiner der beiden Gruppen!

date
[äi]

withdraw
[ah]

gawky for sale prefer airwaves stay
talk gamble solve break landmark

life
[ai]

loud
[au]

time down without could hide
riddled ground lightning tireless counteract

Need to Know *und* The Balance (S. 93–114)

7 Vervollständigen Sie die Sätze mit einem passenden Wort. Es ist jeweils nur eine der angegebenen Möglichkeiten richtig.

Ra's al Ghul instructed the assassins that Batman was not to be ________________.

followed | harmed | cheated | laughed at

One of the shadow assassins calls Batman weak and a ____________ because Batman values life and does not have a killer's heart.

coward | foe | freak | buddy

By scraping some ______________ off the assassin's nose Batman can locate Ra's al Ghul's hiding place.

dirt | blood | skin | sweat

Before Batman can set off for the Pacific, the Batplane needs to be ____________________.

cleaned | refueled | built | found

Ra's al Ghul regularly immerses himself in a healing pool in order to stay ________________.

evil | sacred | preposterous | immortal

Although Talia has been hit by two bullets she has a chance to ________________ because she fell into the healing pool.

be subdued | survive | be loved | slip away

8 Lösen Sie das Kreuzworträtsel, indem Sie die deutschen Begriffe übersetzen.

Die Buchstaben in den markierten Feldern ergeben – richtig zusammengesetzt – den englischen Begriff für den fahrbahren Untersatz des Jokers.

waagerecht:
1 Tumult
3 Notfall
5 böse
7 inserieren
9 klebrig
11 Handschuh
12 Gedanke
13 Rosinen
14 Belegschaft

senkrecht:
2 Freunde
4 Bedürfnisse
6 Rache
8 giftig
10 ersticken

Das Fahrzeug des Jokers ist ein:

☐ ☐ ☐ ☐ ☐ ☐ ☐ ☐ ☐ ☐

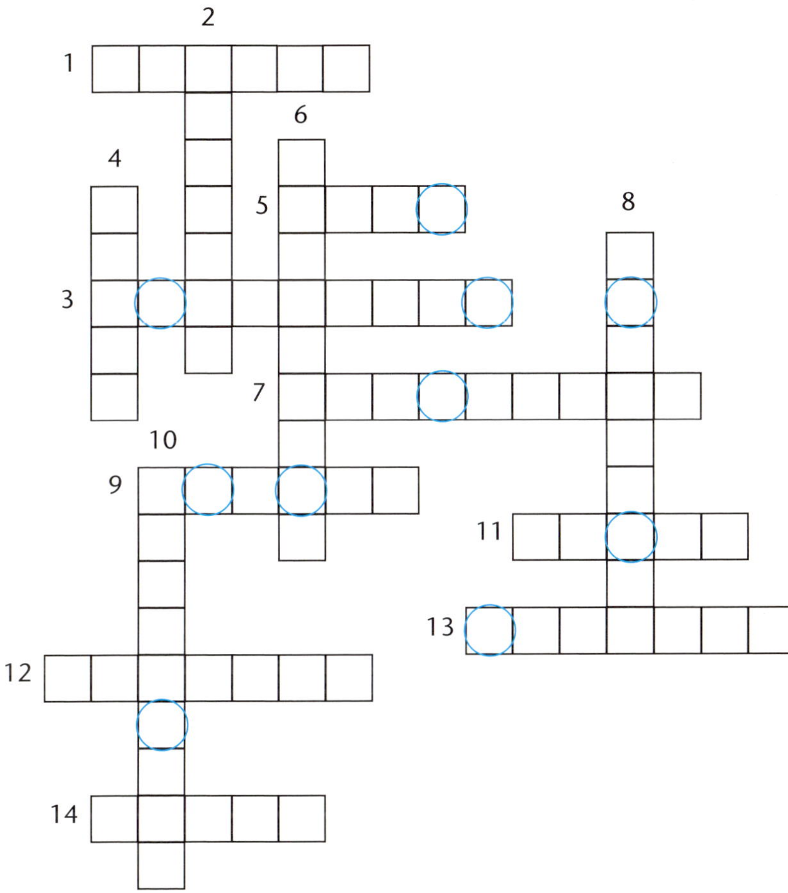
2
1
6
4
5
8
3
7
10
9
11
13
12
14

Lösungen

1

2 1. Catwoman's personal assistant is very angry with Batman and tells him to go back to his cave. **O**

2. Mr. Borodin did not report the stolen Picassos because he did not want to admit that his security system was worthless. **S**

3. The Iceberg Lounge is owned by Oswald Cobblepot. **C**

4. Cobblepot set a trap for Catwoman because she had kept some of the stolen things. **P**

Der umgangssprachliche Ausdruck für „Polizei" lautet
C O P S .

3 federal facility
keeping secrets
bad luck
fire engines
campaign promise

4

1 BODY
2 PROMISE
3 INSULT
4 SEARCHLIGHT
5 ENEMY

6 WALL
7 ENCOURAGING
8 MAYOR
9 INMATES
10 HONEST

5

s	b	q	e	p	l	a	w	y	e	r	s
o	d	f	z	f	a	g	o	u	m	b	a
b	i	a	x	l	f	c	e	a	g	l	e
j	c	s	k	s	r	o	e	t	a	j	w
e	x	s	c	y	i	o	r	i	u	m	p
c	t	i	g	r	d	t	i	t	c	v	s
t	a	g	t	f	e	p	e	z	s	w	h
i	n	n	p	s	l	y	z	g	x	s	i
o	i	m	n	k	g	c	e	o	t	q	d
n	r	e	n	g	a	d	g	e	t	p	e
s	v	n	y	j	w	o	k	d	g	e	r
m	p	t	x	l	a	n	d	m	a	r	k

6

date
[äi]

for sale
airwaves
stay
break

withdraw
[ah]

gawky
talk
solve
landmark

life
[ai]

time
hide
lightning
tireless

loud
[au]

without
down
ground
counteract

7 Ra's al Ghul instructed the assassins that Batman was not to be harmed.

One of the shadow assassins calls Batman weak and a coward because Batman values life and does not have a killer's heart.

By scraping some skin off the assassin's nose Batman can locate Ra's al Ghul's hiding place.

Before Batman can set off for the Pacific, the Batplane needs to be refueled.

Ra's al Ghul regularly immerses himself in a healing pool in order to stay immortal.

Although Talia has been hit by two bullets she has a chance to survive because she fell into the healing pool.

8

Das Fahrzeug des Jokers ist ein:
MOTORCYCLE